THE EVERYTHING KIDS'

Riddles & Brain Teasers Book

Hours of challenging fun!

Kathi Wagner and Aubrey Wagner

Adams Media

Avon, Massachusetts

To Pop, we miss you!

EDITORIAL
Publishing Director: Gary M. Krebs
Managing Editor: Kate McBride
Copy Chief: Laura MacLaughlin
Acquisitions Editor: Bethany Brown
Development Editor: Julie Gutin
Production Editor: Jamie Wielgus

PRODUCTION
Production Director: Susan Beale
Production Manager: Michelle Roy Kelly
Series Designer: Colleen Cunningham
Layout and Graphics: Colleen Cunningham,
    Rachael Eiben, John Paulhus,
    Daria Perreault, Erin Ring
Cover Layout: Paul Beatrice, Frank Rivera

Published by Adams Media, an F & W Publications Company
57 Littlefield Street, Avon, MA 02322. U.S.A.
www.adamsmedia.com

ISBN: 1-59337-036-9

Printed in the United States of America.

J I H G F E D C B A

This publication is designed to provide accurate and authoritative information with regard to the subject matter covered. It is sold with the understanding that the publisher is not engaged in rendering
legal, accounting, or other professional advice. If legal advice or other expert assistance is required,
the services of a competent professional person should be sought.
        — From a *Declaration of Principles* jointly adopted
by a Committee of the American Bar Association and a Committee of Publishers and Associations

Many of the designations used by manufacturers and sellers to distinguish their products are
claimed as trademarks. Where those designations appear in this book and Adams Media was
aware of a trademark claim, the designations have been printed in initial capital letters.

Cover illustrations by Dana Regan.
Interior illustrations by Kurt Dolber and Barry Littmann.
Puzzles by Beth Blair.

Puzzle Power Software by Centron Software Technologies, Inc.
was used to create some puzzle grids.

This book is available at quantity discounts for bulk purchases.
For information, call 1-800-872-5627.

See the entire Everything® series at www.everything.com.

Acknowledgments

We would like to thank Clifford Racine
for taking the time to teach us
what a good laugh is all about.

Contents

Introduction

You may have come to know riddles and brain teasers as a great way to get a good laugh, or maybe to challenge a friend. You may even like to challenge yourself with these riddles. But did you know that thousands of years ago, people just like you were interested in a good riddle or puzzle, too?

Some were interested for different reasons than others, depending on their needs. For instance, one of the first uses for a riddle was to "secretly" carry a message from one person to another—a quiz of sorts that only you knew the answer to, and hopefully the person on the other end would be smart enough to solve or figure out. Unfortunately, not everyone was. For example, one of the most famous riddles of all time was that of Samson from the Bible. As a challenge, Samson tried to trick the Philistines with a riddle about honey. Frustrated and angry, the people decided to solve the riddle of Samson's strength instead. When they discovered the answer, they removed his hair, took away his strength, and defeated him.

Many of the words or expressions in our world are forms of these earlier riddles and brain teasers. Take your name, for example. Did you know that your name has a hidden meaning? The stories behind both our first and last names are usually more than meet the eye. Entire books have been written to explain the original meanings behind any first name. Last names are usually easier to guess, as people used to "sneak" what they did for a living into their last name, such as Smith (for blacksmith or goldsmith) and Wagoner. Or, they would use their father's name and then add the word "son" on the end, as in Johnson and Peterson. And middle names? Well, they hid your family lineage by using your mother's maiden name for your middle name.

Puzzling maybe, but there's more: Do you know which famous author secretly fooled a great number of readers by using his last name spelled backward? Actually, his last name was Geisel, and when he wrote it backward, it became Lesieg . . . but he became famous through his middle name. Do you know what it was? (The answer is at the end of this page.) Authors aren't the only tricksters. Artists and actors, musicians and entertainers also like to challenge us to try to figure out the sometimes-tough riddle of who they are. Or better yet, who they were.

Probably the biggest brain teaser of all is trying to solve the puzzle of the mind itself. Understanding how our brains work has been one of the greatest mysteries ever. Today, the workings of the brain are still a riddle or brain teaser in need of a solution, if you are interested. This book would be a wonderful place for you to start warming up for a mental challenge.

Almost everyone loves a good mystery or puzzle, and puzzles are a fun way of exercising your brain and testing your friends' skills as well. Best of all, riddles and brain teasers are there to be enjoyed. So, prepare to be tricked, tested, riddled, and teased until you can't take any more—and have fun!

—Dr. Seuss (Theodor Seuss Geisel)

Chapter 1
Time for School

brain teaser:

A question or test used to tease and entertain our brains. Some types of brain teasers also stimulate our funny bones. These popular little puzzles or mysteries have been around for a long time.

Why do scissors cut in a line?
They can't stand to wait.

What did Mary tell her little lamb?
Ewe cannot be at school.

Where do elementary school teachers like to go sailing?
Out on the AB seas.

Why couldn't O go to the game?
Because it was too busy minding its Ps and Qs.

How did all the school supplies find their way out of the classroom?
They used the compass.

Which grade keeps the best time?
"Second" grade.

The school janitor has **100 keys** on his ring and can't remember which key opens the front door. What are the odds that he'll find it the first time? **Bonus:** What if he tries 2 keys?

1 in 100. Bonus: The odds are twice as good!

When Johnny **Falls** brought his plant to school for an experiment, nothing he tried could make it grow. Do you know why? **Hint:** His name is part of the clue.

It was fake ("false")

On Tuesday, little **Tommy** was asked to write I AM SORRY FOR WHAT I DID **50** times on a sheet of paper. The last time he was in trouble, he had to write it out **100** times. What do you think about his two offenses?

What he did on Tuesday was only half as bad as what he did the last time

Do you know which letter of the alphabet comes before **R? L? A?**

Q, K, nothing

Try This Try This Try This

Count Me Crazy

Can you count backward from 100 by 6's? It would go like this: 100, 94, 88, 82, 76, 70, 64, 58, 52, 46, 40, 34, 28, 22, 16, 10, 4. Now, try counting backward by 5's, only this time see if you can count backward while walking backward! Careful now, you should be somewhere safe and in the open for this one!

If Carter Elementary School has **2** front doors, **2** back doors, **3** bathroom doors, and **7** classroom doors, how many doors are there "in" the school?

15, counting the indoors

When **Maddy** started school, she was **5** years old. Now that she is in third grade, she is only **6**. How can that be? **Hint:** Maddy's birthday is in February.

Maddy's birthday is on February 29 (it comes only once every 4 years, in a leap year)

What is a wizard's favorite subject?
Spell-ing.

Why is a ruler the most stubborn of your school supplies?
Because it's very narrow-minded.

Why was the English book following the math book around?
He was studying him.

Why did the pair of safety scissors fail her cutting test?
She didn't get the point.

When the police officers arrived at the scene of the crime, how did they know that the numbers, not the letters, were innocent?
It just didn't add up.

Words to Know

riddle:

A question or event of puzzling nature that requires you to think of an answer. Some riddles are a type of joke. Other riddles are really challenging.

What's So Funny?

When Mrs. Spacey's class returned from recess, she seemed very upset. She was sure someone had taken her glasses. "This isn't funny, class!" she scolded as she looked high and low under her desk and all over the room. If only they could stop laughing long enough to get one word out, someone would tell her where they were!

What's so funny?

They were on her head

For an entire week the students in **Mr. Wilson's** science class participated in an experiment to see how many hairs you lose from your head each day. After **1 week** of brushing, the average was around **100** hairs per day. Yet Mr. Wilson's brush was clean. Do you know why?

He was bald

Jennifer's teacher has **17** students in her class. When a new student arrived, she had to change the tables in her room. She used to have **2** medium tables, seating **5**, and **1** large table, seating **7**. Now, if she can also get small tables seating **3**, which tables will she need and how many of them?

Either 3 medium tables and 1 small; or 1 large, 1 medium, and 2 small

During recess, **Alexia** and her friends like to make up codes. Her favorite code uses the letter of the alphabet that comes right after the letter that it actually stands for. Using her code, can you figure out what she wrote in this message?

J MPWF CSBJO UFBTFST.

I LOVE BRAIN TEASERS

Fun Fact

Brain Power
The brain is a mass of tissue located inside your head. Your brain serves as central command control. It's the center of your nervous system and regulates your thoughts, emotions, and the functions of your body.

Why why did did the the history history teacher teacher say say every every thing thing twice twice?
Because history repeats itself.

What is a snake's favorite part of school?
Recesssssssss!

Do you know why the chalk was always yawning?
It was "board."

What will you never find at the end of class?
The head of the class.

Which insect does the best in English class?
The spelling bee.

What do you call a group of strange numbers?
Odd.

There are **30** students in Jake's class. Fifteen of the students have brown hair, **10** of them are blond, and **5** have red hair. If all of the brown-haired students and half of the blonde-haired students have brown eyes, and all of the rest of them have green eyes, how many more students have **brown** eyes than **green**?

Ten more

"Well," said **Mrs. Ray**. "I see **5** people wore ponytails to school today." "Don't you mean **4**, Mrs. Ray?" asked Hannah. Why does Hannah think there are only **4**?

She has forgotten to count herself

Toby likes to climb up the slide at recess. Every time he climbs up **5** feet, he slides back down **2**. How many times does he need to climb up for him to reach 9 feet?

3 times

Try This Try This Try This

Rhyme—No Reason

Do you know how many letters in the alphabet rhyme with the letter B? Eight—C, D, E, G, P, T, V, and Z. Now try making a list of words for your family or friends to try to find a rhyme for. If you want to try an experiment on them, give them 2 sets of lists to try to memorize. One set has 8 words that rhyme, while the other has 8 that do not. Which list will be easier for them to remember?

Bad Band

Begin by writing as many answers as you can under the clues. Then, enter each letter into its numbered box in the answer grid (one has been done for you). Continue working back and forth between the clues and the grid. When you are finished, you will have the answer to the following riddle:

Why was the music teacher so angry during class each day?

1 E	2 F	3 H	4 F	5 A	6 B	7 E		8 F	9 G	10 D
b	e	c	a	u	s	e		t	h	e

	11 E	12 C	13 C	14 G	15 G	16 A	17 I	18 C		
	s	t	u	d	e	N	t	s		

19 F	20 C	21 D	22 H		23 B	24 H	25 I	26 H	27 B	28 D
W	e	r	e		a	l	W	a	y	s

	29 B	30 I	31 F	32 I	33 G	34 C	35 E			
	p	a	s	s	i	n	g			

36 H	37 B	38 D	39 D	40 A						
n	o	t	e	s	!					

A. The center of our solar system

$\underset{40}{S}\ \underset{5}{U}\ \underset{16}{N}$

B. Covered with soap

$\underset{6}{S}\ \underset{37}{O}\ \underset{23}{O}\ \underset{29}{P}\ \underset{27}{Y}$

C. Melodies

$\underset{12}{t}\ \underset{13}{u}\ \underset{34}{n}\ \underset{20}{e}\ \underset{18}{s}$

D. Many of these make a forest

$\underset{38}{t}\ \underset{21}{r}\ \underset{10}{e}\ \underset{39}{e}\ \underset{28}{s}$

E. Pleads

$\underset{1}{b}\ \underset{7}{e}\ \underset{35}{g}\ \underset{11}{s}$

F. Your skin will do this on a hot day

$\underset{31}{S}\ \underset{19}{W}\ \underset{2}{e}\ \underset{4}{a}\ \underset{8}{t}$

G. To put out of sight

$\underset{9}{h}\ \underset{33}{i}\ \underset{14}{d}\ \underset{15}{e}$

H. Opposite of dirty

$\underset{3}{c}\ \underset{24}{l}\ \underset{22}{e}\ \underset{26}{a}\ \underset{36}{n}$

I. How you hit a fly

$\underset{32}{S}\ \underset{25}{W}\ \underset{30}{a}\ \underset{17}{t}$

6

On the playground, **Travis** sees an amazing swing set with **20** swings. While he watches his friends swing, he realizes that as the first swing swings **forward**, the second one swings **back**, the third one swings **forward**, and so on. Which way is the eleventh one swinging?

Forward

For **Erin's** birthday, her mother brought cookies to school. Erin's class has **17** students and **1** teacher, but **3** children were sick that day and **1** went to the dentist. If her mother brought **30** cookies, how many **cookies** did everyone receive?

2 (2 for each child, 2 for the teacher, and 2 for Erin's mother)

Writing Riddles and Brain Teasers

You can write brain teasers and riddles backward, by taking the punchline, or answer, and adding a question to the beginning of it. For example, using the phrase "This is the pits!" you can add the question, "What did one cherry say to the other when he knew it was the end?"

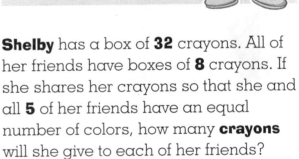

Who am I?

It's my job to ask the puzzling questions, and it's the contestant's job to pick the right answers and win the million dollars. Sometimes, the contestant chooses to phone a friend. **Who am I?**

The host of *Who Wants to Be a Millionaire?*

Shelby has a box of **32** crayons. All of her friends have boxes of **8** crayons. If she shares her crayons so that she and all **5** of her friends have an equal number of colors, how many **crayons** will she give to each of her friends?

4 crayons

Ian likes math class. One day the teacher asks him if he can think of any way that **1 + 1** could equal **1**. Ian was stumped. But in a few minutes, he could think of several ways. Can **you** think of any?

1 person + 1 hamburger, 1 spider + 1 fly, 1 cat + 1 bowl of milk, and so on

A Sloppy Subject

Color in each letter below that appears four times. Collect the uncolored letters from left to right and top to bottom, and write them in the spaces. When you're finished, you'll have the answer to this riddle:

When should kids wear bibs in school?

```
C D H U F
R W I T W
O H F Z N
F G O A O
S Z P H C
T H W I Z
C V L V L
Z I N V G
B W F E O
T E V T C
```

_ _ _ _ _ _ _
_ _ _ _ _ _ _ _ _!

What did one test say to the other?
My life is an open book.

Why did the capital letters have to stay away from the lowercase letters?
They couldn't see "I" to "i" (eye to eye).

How did the playground win the ball game?
The swing swung and the slide slid into home!

What does the alphabet do at the end of the day?
Catch a few more ZZZZZ's.

How did the tooth fairy do in school?
Fairy well.

Why did the fish have to leave school?
He was feeling "eel."

For **Robbie's** class party, the students played musical chairs. Each time the music stopped, Robbie moved over **3** chairs. There were **27** chairs in the circle. How many times did the **music stop** before Robbie was back in his own seat?

9 times

8

Fun Fact

We're Brainiacs

Our brains are made up of billions of cells. And although our brains are a larger part of our bodies compared to most other animals, size has little to do with intelligence. Studies have proven that someone with a small brain can actually be smarter than someone with a larger brain.

Each year **Mrs. Jones's** students bring her apples for the first day of class. Mrs. Jones likes to take the apples home and make pies out of them. If everyone in her class of **21** brings her an apple and it takes **7** apples to make a pie, how many **pies** can she make?

3 pies

What's the difference between **124** and **12**?

The number 4

When Bill added **5** and **5** together, his answer was an **X**. How can that be?

He was using Roman numerals: V + V = X

The monkey bars at **Bobby's** school have **11** bars. If Bobby starts with his right hand on the very first bar, and he skips every other bar as he swings across, while he is changing hands with every other swing, which of his hands will end up on bar **11**? Which one will end up on bar **5**?

His left hand will be on bar 11 and his right on bar 5

Color Me In!

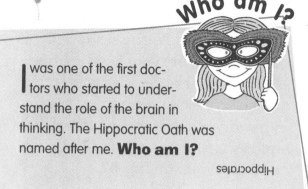

Who am I?

I was one of the first doctors who started to understand the role of the brain in thinking. The Hippocratic Oath was named after me. **Who am I?**

Hippocrates

The most exciting day at **Greenfield School** was the day that the magician came. Everyone could hardly wait for the amazing "pulling the rabbit out of the hat" trick. At the beginning of the show, **Merlin the Mystifying** placed the rabbit in the hat. At the end of the show, even Merlin was amazed. Not only did he pull 1 rabbit out of his hat—he pulled out **6 more!** How could that be?

The mother rabbit had 6 bunnies

Did the math teacher know he would win the annual math contest?

He was counting on it.

Why was the calendar so scared?

His days were numbered.

What kind of school isn't in the front and isn't in the back?

A middle school.

What school did Sherlock Holmes attend?

Elementary, my dear Watson, elementary.

Where do teachers grow their flowers?

In the kinder-gardens.

Why did the computer teacher leave a trap in his room?

Because of the mouse problem.

Try This Try This Try This

Do You Know Your ZYX's?
Can you say the alphabet backward? Z, Y, X, W, V, U, T, S, R, Q, P, O, N, M, L, K, J, I, H, G, F, E, D, C, B, and A. How about an extra added twist? This time, try it while you are listening to music or TV at the same time. Concentration or the lack of it can affect how well we think and learn.

Beth has an unusual talent. She can walk backward for miles. Some days she even walks to school **backward**. If it takes her longer to get there, how much farther is it to **school**?

It isn't any farther—it just takes longer

What would happen if you **8** and **8**?

You'd get a very full stomach (ate and ate)

Fun Fact

A Secret Message
Did you know that before we discovered how funny and silly riddles are, people were actually using them to deliver secret messages? It was also believed that only very bright people would understand the messages or would be able to think of the answers.

Math class

Look at the fraction below each blank. Pick the shape that shows that fraction, using these rules:

Write the letter of that shape on the line. When you are finished, you will have the answer to this riddle:

- The white part of each shape is empty.
- The shaded part of each shape is full.

What do you get when you add 2 bananas, 1 apple, 15 grapes, and ½ melon?

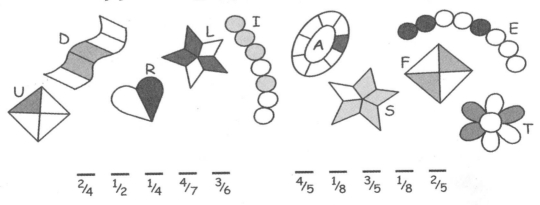

$$\frac{2}{4} \quad \frac{1}{2} \quad \frac{1}{4} \quad \frac{4}{7} \quad \frac{3}{6} \qquad \frac{4}{5} \quad \frac{1}{8} \quad \frac{3}{5} \quad \frac{1}{8} \quad \frac{2}{5}$$

Words to Know

puzzle:

A type of test or challenge sometimes used to confuse someone. Often puzzles are used for learning in school settings, such as language or math lessons. Other types of puzzles are actually objects or games.

In **Mrs. Sharpe's** class, each student has **1** writing instrument, either a pen or a pencil. If there are **21** students in her class and **1/3** use a pen, how many **pencils** are there in class?

14 pencils

As **Elizabeth** wrote the date on her paper, she realized it read **04-04-04**. All three numbers were the same! How many more **years** can this happen in a row?

8 more, until 12-12-12

What did the paper say to the scissors when they kept poking him?
Cut it out!

What did the numbers call the new room in their house?
Their addition.

Why do rabbits do so well in school?
They like to multiply.

What do you get when you put 2 500-pound elephants on a teeter-totter?
A broken teeter-totter!

Why did everyone think their teacher was so special?
She had a lot of "class."

What do you call numerals that don't feel anything?
"Numb"ers.

Why didn't the pencil do well on his test?
He wasn't very sharp.

Just for fun, **Cassie** taught her cat Freddie sign language. One day the cat tapped on the window (a sign for **"bird"**), tapped his tail on the wall (a sign for **"mouse"**), and jumped into the tub to swim (a sign for **"fish"**). What was Freddie trying to tell Cassie?

"I'm hungry."

When the **circus** comes to town Bobby always goes to see it. His favorite part is when the elephants build a pyramid. "Can you believe it?" asks the announcer. "A record **21 ELEPHANTS**!" Amazed, Bobby starts counting: 1 on top, 2 below it, 3 more below them, and so on. If the announcer is right, how many elephants will be on the **bottom** row?

6 elephants

What do you call 2 half rabbits put together?
A rabbit "whole."

What do you call a really strange anteater?
An "odd-vark."

Why did the stallion need a cough drop?
He was hoarse.

What Beatles song do fish everywhere love?
"Twist and Trout."

What do you get when you cross Sir Lancelot with a horse?
A "knight-mare."

What did one cat call the other when he wouldn't play fair?
Cheetah!

Words to Know

joke:

A joke is an act or statement that causes laughter. Funny riddles are a type of joke.

Fun Fact

Tickle Me Fun
Did you know it is impossible for
you to tickle yourself? It's true; one of
the things needed in tickling is the element of
surprise—not expecting to be tickled. Not sure?
Try it for yourself.

One night **Tommy** had a bad dream.
There was a bull chasing him all
around the arena, but just as the **bull**
was about to ram him, Tommy got
away. Do you know how?

He woke up

What is **bald** but has its head covered?

The bald eagle

Which one of these **does not belong**
in the group—shark, whale, and
swordfish?

The whale, because it's a mammal

Which one of these **does not belong** to
the set? Lion, tiger, elephant, and polar
bear.

The elephant, because he has no fur

Egg is to **chicken** as acorn is to what?

A tree

When a small **campground** was
robbed last week, the police brought
the only witness in for a line-up. All of
the **animals** were brought in and
placed in a line. When it came time for
the witness to point out the bandit, she
said she couldn't be sure which one
had done it, because the robber looked
like he was wearing a **mask**. Do you
know who it was?

The raccoon

**An Anagram of
Your Own**
Have you ever tried to
make your own anagrams?
An anagram is a word or
phrase formed by recording the
letters of another word or phrase,
like "late" and "tale." How many
anagrams can you and your
friends come up with?

Loop the Zoo!

Find the path through the zoo that takes Zack to three of his favorite animals. Along the way, collect the letters that spell out three different answers to this riddle: What goes black, white, black, white, black, white?

Where does a mother robin keep her money?

In a nest egg.

What do cows do for fun?

They go to the "moo-vies."

How do sheep go to sleep?

They count people.

Why was the cow so excited when a horse moved in next door?

He had never had a "neigh-bor" before.

What was the last thing the frog did before he jumped?

He croaked.

What time is it when you sit on your cat?

Time to get a new one.

Words to Know

pun:

A pun is a play on words using two meanings of the same word or two words that sound the same but are spelled differently. For example, the word "sew" in the following joke: "Why do I have to?" the little sewing machine asked his mother. "Because I said SEW!" she replied.

Take a look at the following sentence: **"Ants** busily crawl, doing everything **fast."** What's special about it?

The words are in alphabetical order by first letter

Fish swim and **birds** fly, but does it ever happen the other way around? Do birds ever **swim** and do fish ever **fly**? Can you think of any examples?

Penguins swim; flying fish can fly for short periods of time

Andrew has amazing pets. His dogs and cats would get along, but they **eat** each other's food. How does Andrew keep this from happening?

He feeds the dogs during the day, while the cats are sleeping; he feeds the cats during the night, while the dogs are asleep

17

What do horses have at night?

"Night-mares."

What do you call 2 insects that raise their young?

"Pair-ants."

Why did the fox sell his fur?

Because he "pelt" like it.

Why does the duck walk everywhere he goes?

Because he can't drive.

Why shouldn't you make a tired canine tell the truth?

Because you're supposed to let sleeping dogs lie.

Do possums really hang upside down from trees all night?

It's a "possum-bility."

One day, **cows** from the Busy "B" ranch and cows from the Lazy "1" ranch got all mixed up. The ranch **cowboys** were confused. How can they tell the cows **apart** in order to separate them?

Most cows are branded, so they should look for a "B" or a "1" brand on each cow

When the **circus** came to town, everyone was surprised—even the lion tamer, as he discovered **7** new lion cubs in the lion cage. Before long, everyone agreed it would be best to separate the feisty **cubs**. But how? Then the ringmaster had an idea: "I know a way you can place **3** large rings to make **7** sections, one for each cub." Do you know how to do that?

Place the first 2 rings so that one slightly overlaps the other—that's 3 sections; then, place the third ring in the center of the 2, to make 7 sections

Who am I?

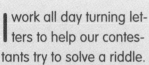

I work all day turning letters to help our contestants try to solve a riddle.
Not only do they have a "wheely" good time, but they also have a chance to win a "fortune." **Who am I?**

Vanna White from Wheel of Fortune

What do you get when you wake a sleeping bear?
Trouble!

What are three words you never say to a raccoon?
Coonskin cap.

What do you call a really picky cat?
A "paw-ticular" feline.

How can you tell when a polar bear is moving?
There's a "fur sale" sign in the yard.

What do you give to a 500-pound alligator when he knocks at your door?
Anything he wants.

How do fish finish their floors?
They "carp it."

Say What?

On each line, add the first and last letter to complete the name of the animal that is suggested by what that animal is saying. Then, read DOWN the shaded column to answer this riddle:

What is it that camels have that no other animals have?

_RA_	"I'm grouchy!"
AND	"Where's the bamboo?"
_U_	"I'll grow up to be a big bear!"
ONKE	"Got a banana?"
_RO_	"-odile is the last part of my name!"
YEN	"Ha, Ha, Ha!"
_OR_	"You won't like me in your apple!"
NAK	"What'ssssss up?"
_W_	"Whoooo's there?"
_AT_	"Turn out the light! We like the dark!"

Take the Laughing Test
How do you think you would do on a laughing test? To try the challenge, record someone laughing, then play back the tape to see if you can keep from laughing yourself. They say laughter is contagious. Can you come up with laughing tests of your own?

A **vet** has 10 sick **hamsters**, 10 sick **dogs**, and 10 ill **cats**. Unfortunately, he can't leave them alone as they are not too sick for the dogs to attack the cats, and the cats to try to eat the hamsters. At the end of the day he decides to take them home to **keep an eye** on them. What is the smallest number of trips he can make across town and how?

2: On the first trip he takes the cats and on the second trip he takes the dogs and the hamsters

What do **stripes, mane, tail,** and **hooves** have in common?

They're all traits of a zebra

Which **creature** doesn't belong—**wasp, bee, spider, or ant**?

The spider—it's an arthropod, not an insect

Birds and fish are to **worms** as cats and snakes are to **what**?

Mice—birds and fish eat worms; cats and snakes eat mice

What do you call a sleeping baby goat?
A "kid napping."

What happens when you blend a reptile with a back street?
You get an "alley-gator."

What travels faster than the speed of dog?
A cat!

Why was the rabbit so excited about her engagement ring?
It was 5 carrots!

Why did they take Polly away?
She went crackers!

What did the giraffe say when he bent down to talk to the fish?
LONG time no sea.

Feel Better

A riddle and its answer were put into the large grid, and then cut into eight pieces. See if you can figure out where each piece goes, and write the letters in their proper places. When you have filled the grid in correctly, you will be able to read the puzzle from left to right, and top to bottom. HINT: The black boxes stand for the spaces between words.

?			A
N	T	!	

S		A	T
G	E	T	-

A	N	D
E	R	S
M	A	L

	T	H	E
W	E	L	L

'	S		G
N	G	S	
S	I	C	K

R	A	Y	
F	L	O	W
	A	N	I

W	H	A	T
	B	R	I
	T	O	

	Z	O	O
E	P	H	A

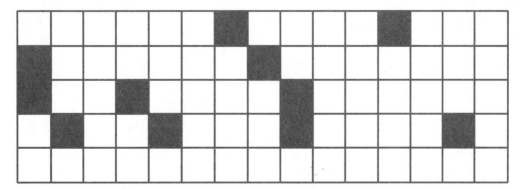

When **Mini's** family pulled up at the motel, Mini, her parents, and **12** brothers and sisters poured out of the car. How **could** that happen?

Mini and her family are mice.

What do a **shark,** a **mouse,** and a **mole** have in common?

All of their babies are called "pups."

Fun Fact

A Human Survival Guide
Over time people have studied how the human brain and body work together. One thing your brain knows is that you need at least 5 things to survive—water, food, oxygen, shelter, and clothing.

Where do hogs go when they need a loan?
To the piggy bank.

What did one mouse say to the other mouse who held the door open for him?
Why, that was very "mice" of you!

What did one python say to the other before they made a deal?
Let's "snake" on it.

Why did the cub get in trouble with his mother?
She caught him "lion."

Why couldn't the dog say, "Ahhh"?
Because the cat got his tongue.

The minute **Rastus** laid eyes on the rattlesnake, it lunged at him, but it could not bite the **boy.** Can you guess **why?**

Rastus was at a zoo and the snake was behind glass

What's So Funny?

When Ted arrived home one evening, he was startled by a bear in his yard! After his initial panic, he stopped and breathed a sigh of relief. The bear was no danger to him at all! **What's so funny?**

The bear was stuffed

Chapter 3

Travel the World

Words to Know

enigma:

An enigma is a phrase or question that is confusing or hard to understand. Enigmas or riddles have been used throughout time to test one's ability to solve a puzzle or mystery.

How did the snow pile get across the sea?

It went a-drift.

What did the P. E. teacher ride in to the ball?

A coach.

How did the train engine know he was lost?

He was on the wrong side of the tracks.

How long does it take for a person to fly to Chicago?

People can't fly, silly!

What kind of water greets you?

An ocean wave.

What does a train say when it has a cold?

Ahhh Choo-Choo!

When the **storm** hit and the **plane** attempted to land, everyone in the air and on the ground was speechless. Yet somehow they **communicated** the directions to land. How?

They used signals

What do the **stop light, fire truck,** and **stop sign** have in common?

They're all red

When **Anna's** family decided to take a vacation, everyone wanted to go. So Anna, her **mom** and **dad**, her two **brothers**, their **Aunt** Lucille, their **Uncle** Ed, and **Grandma** rode the bus together all the way from New York to California and back again. How many **people** in all made the trip?

9, including the bus driver

Who am I?

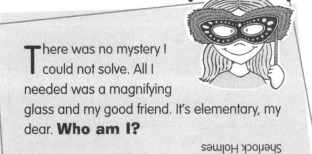

There was no mystery I could not solve. All I needed was a magnifying glass and my good friend. It's elementary, my dear. **Who am I?**

Sherlock Holmes

What do you call an imaginary yacht?
A dream boat.

How did the dentist get across the river?
With a "tooth ferry."

How do you fasten a railroad track together?
With a railroad tie.

What do you call an angry ship?
A steamed boat.

When does a truck sleep?
When it gets "tire-d."

What is the opposite of a put-down?
A pick-up.

When **Juan's** plane left the ground it was **2 P.M.** After flying for **2** hours, it landed—but the clocks at the airport showed that it was *still* **2 P.M.** How can this be?

The airplane flew through 2 time zones

If **three** friends moved to the same town, and one lived on **E-X** Avenue, while another lived on **E-Y** Road, where does the third one live?

E-Z Street

What **doesn't** belong? Snow skis, Jet Ski, bus, motorcycle.

The Jet Ski—it's the only one that doesn't travel on land

Fun Fact

Laughing Out Loud
Did you know that the older you get, the less you laugh? Babies laugh on and off all day long, while someone who is older may laugh only once a day. Now, make sure you don't miss your chance to laugh your head off!

Do you know what a watch does on vacation?

Time travel.

What did the space travelers eat on their flight?

Astro-nuts.

What's the last thing you see when a train goes by?

Its tracks.

Why wouldn't the police officer cross the road?

Because the light wasn't green.

Why did the army sergeant's car die?

Because its "tank" was empty.

What do accountants ride in?

A "tax-i."

Words to Know

amusement:

What people do or use in order to entertain themselves or someone else. Silly or fun things are used to amuse people every day.

What's So Funny?

Ike the famous bike rider pedaled for hours on his bike only to find that he was right back where he started. **What's so funny?**

He was on his exercise bike at the gym!

What **doesn't belong** in this list? Pen, paper, spatula, notebook.

Spatula

Joey and his sister **Hannah** like to play "I Spy" when they travel in the car. They decide that this time the first person who "spies" the most legs on the trip wins! Joey sees 2 **deer**, 11 cows, 2 **cats**, and a spider. Hannah sees 1 turkey, 7 **cows**, 3 sheep, and 4 **cats**. Who won?

Joey with 68 to Hannah's 58

The class was really **puzzled** when the teacher asked them: "When can you see through the **desert**?" Do you know?

When it is heated to almost 3,000 degrees and the sand becomes glass

Funny Flight

"I just flew home from Paris, and..."

First, figure out what word each picture puzzle represents. Then put the words in the proper order to finish what this silly traveler is saying. Write the numbers in the upper lefthand corner of each picture.

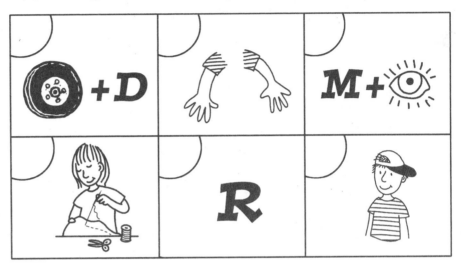

What did the thief get when he stole the tram?

Bus-ted!

What does an elephant always take on safari?

His trunk.

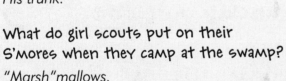

What do girl scouts put on their S'mores when they camp at the swamp?

"Marsh"mallows.

Where does dinnerware go on vacation?

To China.

As **Mrs. Rockefeller** was leaving the airport, she found herself accidentally trapped in the revolving **glass doors**. She had no luggage, no tools, and nobody was around. She eventually made a **hole** and escaped. How? **Hint: Her name.**

She cut a hole in the glass with her diamond ring

No matter how long the new department **store clerk** walked down the stairs, he could never seem to reach the basement. **Why?**

He was walking down the "up" escalator

Where in the World?

First unscramble the names of eight different places around the world.
Then match each one to a riddle to discover eight popular vacation spots!

1. Where do fish go on vacation?
2. Where do songbirds go on vacation?
3. Where do zombies go on vacation?
4. Where do Thanksgiving birds go on vacation?
5. Where do geometry teachers go on vacation?
6. Where do locksmiths go on vacation?

nliFnad   hTe ranCay nsIlsad

eruTky   ehT edaD aSe

auCb   heT arlFoid seKy

Who am I?

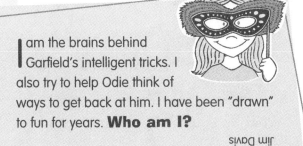

I am the brains behind Garfield's intelligent tricks. I also try to help Odie think of ways to get back at him. I have been "drawn" to fun for years. **Who am I?**

Jim Davis

Sydney and Sadie are cousins. One day, Sydney and Sadie went on vacation to Japan. Sadie's flight took 7 hours while Sydney's took 33. Both flights were nonstop and Sydney and Sadie both left home at the same time from the same city in California. How can this be?

Sadie's plane flew west; Sydney's plane flew east

If flying to California takes **1 ½** hours, and flying to Texas takes **2**, and flying to Hawaii takes **twice as long** as a trip to both places, how long is your flight to Hawaii?

7 hours

What **vehicle** travels over the **ground** at speeds much **faster** than a car but can also go through mountains?

A train

Where do skydivers put their laundry?
In the "para-chute."

What did the child say to the captain when their boat hit rough waters?
I can't steer this, "canoe"?

Where do restless travelers like to go?
To Rome.

What place do worms like to visit the most?
The Big Apple.

What is one way to save money when you go to the lake?
Buy a "sale boat."

Why did the plant get lost on its trip?
It took the wrong "root."

How does a baby beetle get around?
In a buggy.

What do you call it when a highway stumbles?
A road trip.

How does milk travel around?
In a "car ton."

What does a skunk's car run on?
Fumes.

How does Robin Hood get from here to there?
In an "arrow plane."

Stare Me Down
Have you ever tried having a stare down contest? It's fun and easy. All you need is a friend and a lot of concentration. While sitting straight across from your friend, your challenge is to see who can stare into the other person's eyes the longest without blinking or laughing. It's that easy . . . or is it?

If April showers bring May flowers, what do May flowers bring?

Pilgrims

What can **travel** all over the world, without anyone **seeing** it?

The wind

What do the **words** yield, walk, merge, and slow have in **common?**

They're all street signs

Fun Fact

A Hypo What?
The hypothalamus gland in your brain is the reason you can laugh or find some things funny. It also controls your other emotions. One other interesting thing the hypothalamus does is remind your brain to stay awake.

The Hungry Traveler

The following riddle is missing 12 important letters! See if you can fit the letters from the box into the correct blanks. To create an ending that fits this silly story, unscramble the letters in the second box, and fit them into the blanks. HINT: You will use some of the letters more than once!

B C G L M P S U V W Y

A h_n_r_ tra_e_er _a_ takin_ a dri_e thro_ _h the _o_ntr_ _ide. He had _ro_ _ht a _a_ad _ith hi_, _ _t for_ot an i_ _ortant too_. The h_n_r_ tra_e_er fi_ _red he _o_ _d eat _ _n_ h _hen he _ot to a _ertain kind of inter_e_tion. _hat _a_ the h_n_r_ tra_e_er _aitin_ for?

A D E F H I K N O R T

A fork in The road!

Car, tricycle, scooter, and wheelbarrow. What is **special** about this group?

Their order—4 wheels, 3 wheels, 2 wheels, and 1

When **Bartholomew** went to the beach, he found an item that was strong enough to hold a **rock**, but unable to hold **water**. Do you know what this mystery **item** was?

A sieve

Why did the motorcycle stop by the side of the road?
It was "two tire-d" to go on.

What did the mother river name her baby?
Brook.

How do stones get where they are going?
They rock-it.

What do puppies like to ride in?
Waggins.

What do you get when you cross 2 curlers with 2 butter knives?
A pair of roller-blades.

Try This Try This Try This

Write Your Own Comic Strip
If you like to read the "funny pages" or comics in the newspaper, you know a picture or comic can make you laugh. But have you ever tried to make your own comic strip? Learning how to draw or make comics can be a lot of fun. Try it on a rainy day—or try it today!

When the night **guards** found a tourist unconscious on the ground, they were unsure of who he was or whom to **contact**. Eventually, at the hospital, they "developed" a plan. **What was it?**

They processed the film from his camera

Who am I?

Some say the way that I solved the biggest escape puzzle of all time was simply magic. I like to think it was because I used my brain. **Who am I?**

Harry Houdini

Chapter 4
Food and Drink

Words to Know

conundrum:

A conundrum is a riddle that has a pun (or something with two different meanings) for the answer. Here's an example: Why was the letter B in a boat? He was going out to C. But there's another meaning to "conundrum"—it could also be a dilemma or a problem that cannot be solved.

When is a riddle not a riddle?
When you put a "G" in front of it (griddle).

What do you call really scared pasta?
Chicken noodles.

What can rise without ever sleeping?
Bread.

If your dog's down, what's your cat?
Catsup.

Why did the coffee cup go down to the police station?
To report that he had been mugged.

How did the police officers help him?
They showed him several mug shots.

What's the next word?
Dirt, worm, bird, _____.

Cat (it's a food chain)

Once upon a time, a little girl dressed in **blue** went to her grandmother's **Swiss cottage**. Why?

She was hungry for some cheese

When **Sara** invited some friends over to watch a movie, her parents decided to order **pizza** for all of them. When the delivery came, there were **2** large pizzas and **1** small one. If a large pizza serves **8** people and a small pizza serves **4**, how many friends were at Sara's house?

7 friends (20 servings minus 3 for Sara and her parents)

Fun Fact

What's Your IQ?

Your IQ or Intelligence Quotient is arrived at by measuring your chronological age with your mental age. The average score is around 100. The score of a genius will average around 40 to 50 points higher.

Writing on the Wall

Over time researchers have found that no two people have the same handwriting, just like no two people have the same fingerprints. If you study a few samples of other people's handwriting, you may also discover that handwriting can sometimes reveal personality traits. For example, those who separate their letters may be artistic and independent, while those whose letters are very close together might enjoy some company.

When there was a knock at the **door**, a man who could not **see** and could not **hear** somehow knew that someone had left him apple pie outside. **How did he know?**

He could smell it

Jill left a solid object on the **floor** of her room for 3 hours. In those 3 hours, no one had touched it, and yet it completely **disappeared** on its own. What was the object?

An ice cube

What do you call a giggling field of corn?
Laughing stalks.

What does Count Dracula use to cut his food?
A "stake" knife.

What kind of food is sick all the time?
Wheat germ.

When 2 eggs were placed in a blender, the first egg asked, "What's going on here?" What did the second egg say?
"Beats me."

How does bread get up in the morning?
It rises.

Why do melons rarely marry?
They "cantaloupe" (can't elope).

Cucumbers, carrots, onions, tomatoes, and peas—which one **doesn't** belong?

Tomatoes, because they are fruit

One day **Katherine** decided to make a picture out of **food**, just for fun. First she used strawberries, then oranges, then lemons, then kiwis, then blueberries, and then another fruit. What did she use **last** and **why?**

Purple grapes—she was making a fruity rainbow

Let's Play Charades

One sure way to get everyone laughing is to start up a game of charades. The next time you get together with family or friends, try acting out one of these: Fun house mirrors, riding a roller-coaster, buying new shoes, shopping for groceries, and running a race. Can you think of any other fun charades?

What do trees eat their ice cream out of?
Pinecones.

Why did the knife cross the road?
Because there was a fork in it.

What do you call a little potato?
Small fry.

What do you get when a bunch of grapes tries to cross a highway?
A traffic jam.

How does a cucumber know when it's in trouble?
It's in a pickle.

What drink always comes to your rescue?
Lemon-aide.

What type of **food** can contain all of the **food groups?**

Pizza!

Frosting, platter, candles, and sprinkles—what's **missing?**

Birthday cake

frightened food

Use a colored marker to highlight each of the 30 foods stuffed into this letter grid. The words can go sideways, up and down, diagonal, and even backward! After you have found them all, collect the unused letters from TOP to BOTTOM and LEFT to RIGHT, and write them in order on the blank spaces provided. When you're finished, you'll have the answer to this riddle:

EXTRA FUN: Use three different colors of highlight markers to show your answers!

APPLE
BEET
BLINTZ
BREAD
BROWNIES
CAKE
CARROT
CHEESE
CLAM
EGG
HAMBURGER
HOTDOG
JELLY
KIWI
MILK
ORANGE
PEA
PEANUT BUTTER
PEAR
PEPPER
PIE
PIZZA
PLUM
PORK
RADISH
SALAD
SPAGHETTI
TUNA FISH
TURKEY
YAM

What has bread on both sides and is easy to frighten?

S	P	A	G	H	E	T	T	I	E	I	P
E	G	N	A	R	O	U	A	P	P	L	E
A	B	C	S	E	I	N	W	O	R	B	A
C	L	A	M	P	Y	A	M	R	C	E	N
H	I	K	R	L	I	F	K	K	C	E	U
K	N	E	A	U	M	I	L	K	C	T	T
A	T	E	E	M	W	S	A	L	A	D	B
P	Z	U	P	I	H	H	J	G	R	C	U
E	N	Z	R	S	D	S	E	O	R	H	T
P	A	N	I	K	A	D	L	D	O	E	T
P	W	D	I	P	E	C	L	T	T	E	E
E	A	G	G	E	R	Y	Y	O	H	S	R
R	E	G	R	U	B	M	A	H	P	E	A

_ _ _ _ _ _ _ _ _ _ _ _ _ _ _ _ _ _ _!

37

Every night when **Pop** came home, as he opened his door a light came **on**, and as he closed it, the light went **off**. **Why?**

Pop was a soda, and his home was the refrigerator!

What's going on here?

Cup	Plate
Fork	Knife
Spoon	Napkin
Glass	Saucer

The second word in each pair begins with the same letter as the last letter of the first word

Daniel took a piece of **bread**, and on top of that he placed a slice of **tomato**. Next, he added a piece of **lettuce**, a slice of **meat**, and a piece of **cheese**. Do you know what he made?

A food pyramid

Good Home Cookin'

Start at the letter marked with a dot. As you spiral into the center of the shell, collect every other letter. Write them in order on the lines below. When you reach the middle, head back out again, collecting all the letters that you skipped over the first time. Write these letters in order on the lines. When you are finished, you will have the answer to this riddle:

Where does a snail like to eat lunch?

_____ _____ _____!

What's So Funny?

When Chelsea ordered a cheeseburger at Burgers-R-Us, she waited patiently while Calvin carefully added the pickles, onion, cheese, ketchup, mustard, lettuce, and tomato. Just as she was about to take a bite, Calvin yelled, "Wait a minute!" **What's so funny?**

He left the burger out!

In **cooking** class the teacher asked for volunteers. Each volunteer had to answer a question. When it was **Amy's** turn, the teacher asked her what the difference was between **freezing** and **boiling**. Amy used the examples of ice cubes and hot cocoa. Although her teacher thought those were good examples, it wasn't the answer she was looking for. **Do you know the answer?**

180 degrees

What's a pig's favorite way to cook?
Bakin' (bacon).

What did the potato call his son?
Chip.

What does a hog do in the sun?
Roast.

What do mugs build their homes out of?
"Cup boards."

Why were the cups and the forks all alone?
Because the dish ran away with the spoon.

What did the syrup call her sweetheart?
Honey.

When **Ben** and his father went to the grocery store, his father asked him if he could find **4 foods** in the store that had holes in them but that were still whole. Ben found more than 4. **How many** can you think of?

Doughnuts, macaroni, bagels, olives, crackers, and Swiss cheese are just a few possible answers

Who am I?

"To be or not to be" is my hint of who I am. I could also mention Romeo and Juliet. I am well known for my plays as well as my poems. **Who am I?**

William Shakespeare

Second Helping

Place each of the seven-letter words into the boxes in alphabetical order, starting with the top row and working your way to the bottom.

When you're finished, read down the third column to get the answer to this riddle:

What food tastes better before it is cooked?

For a second helping of laughs, read down the fourth column to get the answer to this riddle:

What did the teddy bear say after eating a really big meal?

1.
2.
3.
4.
5.
6.
7.
8.
9.
10.

AQUATIC   COLLAGE

MISERLY   OUTDOOR

GOOFUPS

CONSENT   LOAFERS

ALBINOS

ESTUARY   CARMINE

When **Ozzy** and his friend **Owen** went to tour their local greenhouse, the florist had a mystery for them to solve. "When is a **flower** not a flower?" the florist asked. Do you know the answer?

When it's flour.

What is a **liquid** outside your fridge and a **solid** inside your fridge**?**

Flavored gelatin

What do comic book characters like to eat?
Superhero sandwiches.

What did the other groceries say when the sausage brought the salami to the party?
Well, he's bratwurst (brought worse).

Why were the windows "shuttering"?
Because they heard the homeowners say it was "curtains" for them!

What do you call a naughty glove?
A bad mitten.

When the builder had to climb onto the roof, did he pick the first thing he saw (the scaffolding) or the second thing?
He chose the ladder (latter).

Try This   Try This   Try This

Now I See It, Now You Don't
The way the brain sees things is not always the same from one person to the next. Some people don't see color the same way as others. One way to check for color blindness is to find 4 socks, each one with a different shade of green. Can you tell the difference between the 4 colors? People who are color-blind cannot see the minor differences in the color.

What do cherubs serve at their parties?
Angel food cake.

Who's going to make the salad?
Let us (lettuce)!

What bear can grow 10 times its own size overnight?
A gummy bear in water.

Why wouldn't the apple join the other fruits in the salad?
She didn't find it as a-peeling.

Did you hear that the ice cream parlor closed?
Yeah, I heard that the sundaes wouldn't work on weekdays, the ice cream bars went nuts, and the bananas split.

When **Ed's** mother called out, "Ed, supper is ready!" **4 people** came. Who were they?

Four generations of Eds—Ed I, Ed II, Ed III, and Ed IV

It goes in **fast**, but comes out **slow**—and yet, the amount is the same. **What can this be?**

A funnel

Every day a strange man walked past several **grapevines** growing on a fence. One very **hot** day the owner asked the strange man what he had done with his grapes. "I did not take your grapes," replied the strange man, "I am innocent!" The strange man was telling the **truth**, yet the grapes were gone. Can you solve the **mystery?**

The owner's grapes had turned to raisins in the hot sun

Chapter 5
Acting Silly

Try This · Try This · Try This · Try This

Front to Back—and Back Again
Have you ever tried to write a palindrome? Palindromes are words or phrases that read the same both forward and backward. "Dad" is a good example. Another is "Madam, I'm Adam." How many palindromes can you think of?

How did **Sonny** know his son would be home **soon**?

He added another O

What do you get when you put **.14** and **3** together? The answer is as easy as **pie . . .**

3.14

One night as the **children** were walking past the Parch house, a thick **fog** set in. Cold and scared, the children moved on down the street. Then as **quickly** as it had appeared, the fog ended, and there was no other fog anywhere in sight. **How can that be?**

It was Halloween and the "fog" came from dry ice

What do kindergarten teachers eat for lunch?
Alphabet soup.

How do you make a riddle stop?
You take away its "r" and "d" (idle).

What did the PE teacher name his son?
Gym (Jim).

Why couldn't the geometry teacher solve her own problems?
She didn't have the right angle.

Why did all the letters have to stay after school?
They were caught making "alpha bets."

What did the sleeping pines do?
They knotted off.

You never write on what paper?
Toilet paper.

What happens if you stand when you sleep?

You dream "up" things.

What is the difference between being a fool and being foolish?

4 letters (a & ish).

What is something only two brains can have?

A brain baby.

How many chickens does it take to make a pillow?

None, chickens can't sew!

Where does little bear keep his things at school?

In his cubby.

What do you call just one nap?

A sleep.

Fun Fact

Double-Sided

Did you know that your brain has two sides? The left side of the brain is in charge of things like art and picturing things in your head. The right side is in charge of things like speech, math, and language. Sometimes one side is stronger than the other. Which is your stronger side?

If Sheldon sells **shells** by the shore, and Dora drums drums by the **door**, then who sits on **sofas** on Saturdays? Is it Julie, Laura, Sophie, or Erin?

Sophie (because her name begins with "s").

Tightrope, trapeze, water slide, and cannon—which one **doesn't** belong in this group?

The water slide (it belongs at a swimming pool, not a circus).

"Silly **Sally** sings songs as silly Sammy somersaults." Can you say this **5 times** fast? Can you make up your own **tongue twister?**

tongue twister:

Words to Know

A word or phrase that is hard to repeat quickly due to the repetition of multiple consonants within the words.

comic contest

These four people have entered into a comic contest. Count the number of not-quite-normal things you can see about each contestant's costume and pet. For example, contestant number 1 is wearing a "baseball" cap. The winner has the most comic accessories! Make your lists in the spaces below.

Try This Try This Try This

Brains of Jell-O

Do you know anyone who's so silly, it's like he's got a brain full of Jell-O? Now you can make one yourself. Take a batch of cookie dough and press it down in a bowl, making two big dents (for brain lobes) in it. Cover your dough mold with plastic wrap, making sure it's completely protected, and then pour prepared liquid Jell-O inside. Refrigerate your Jell-O brain for several hours. When the Jell-O hardens, you can move it from the cookie mold to a platter, and use the cookie dough to make brain cookies to go with the Jell-O.

For **Daddy's** birthday, Victoria helped Mommy bake a birthday **cake**. When Mommy walked away for a moment, she told Victoria, "Don't forget to put in the **flour**." So she did. When Mommy came back, she couldn't stop **laughing**. What did she find?

There was a daisy in the mixing bowl

Silly Sally can turn around **25** times in **2** minutes. If she wants to break the town record of **37** minutes of spinning, how many **times** will she need to **spin?**

475 times

What's the **missing word** in the last pair? Little lightning bugs, small snails, mini mice, ___ turtles.

Tiny

Ever since **Dan** got dressed this morning, he's had the strangest feeling that he's going the **wrong way**. Do you know why?

His clothes are on backward

What has 10 fingers on each hand?
A pair of gloves.

Who is the only person the tooth fairy won't visit at night?
Count Dracula.

What would the Count say if she did?
"Fang you" very much.

Why couldn't the jester get his medicine bottle open?
It was "fool" proof.

What did Pinocchio say when he was asked if he was lying?
Who nose?

How much sleep did the insomniac get?
Nod a wink.

47

Who am I?

Many still believe I had the greatest mind of all time. My theory of relativity was the beginning of many new inventions that we have today. Science was my favorite subject. **Who am I?**

Albert Einstein

What is a woodpecker's favorite dessert?

"Tap-ioca" pudding.

What object in space is never hungry?

The full moon.

What does Cyclops drink out of?

Eye glasses.

What type of fishing do the Three Billy Goats Gruff like to do?

Trolling.

What did the mother bolt say to her baby when she tucked him in bed?

Sleep tight.

What's the difference between April 1st and April 2nd?

One day.

When **Nate** told his mother that he could turn an open bottle filled with water **upside down** and the water would not pour out, she said, "I'll believe it when I see it." And she did. What did Nate do in order **to keep** the water in the bottle?

The bottle was in a tub of water and he never raised it higher than the opening of the bottle.

One day Backward **Betty** decided to try a mud bath like the stars take. The nearest **mud puddle** she could find was in the neighbor's driveway. As Betty began to bathe, something seemed strange. **What was wrong?**

It wasn't mud—it was cement

Fun Fact

Sizing Up Your Brain

In the past, some experts wondered if the size of your brain decided how smart you could be. Now they know that it's not really true. But here's another fact—did you know that the size of your head compared with your body changes considerably as you grow? At birth, your head is 1/4 of your body size. By the time you're an adult, your body catches up and your head is only 1/10 of your body.

"**Jack** and **Jill** went down a hill to fetch a pail of dirt. Jill fell down and broke her foot, and Jack came tumbling after. What's **wrong** with this story?

Everything is backward

When it was finally **Mr. Smiley's** turn at the Laughs-R-on-Us booth, they told him he had better take his **turn** now, as they were about to run out. So what did Mr. Smiley get?

The last laugh

Color Us In!

Silly Sally

Can you guess what Silly Sally likes? Take a look at the following clues:

Silly Sally likes...

...noodles, but not ravioli

...meatballs, but not hotdogs

...trees, but not bushes

...riddles, but not jokes

EXTRA FUN: The picture of Silly Sally shows several things that Sally likes. Can you figure out what they are, and why?

Silly Slogans

Write each numbered word in the correct box. Now, rearrange the words to finish the silly slogan for each business!

1. a	3. in	5. look	4. bright	3. cuts!	1. deal!
4. a	6. looking	3. ...are	1. ...want	6. sale!	3. all
2. ...knead	3. short	6. a	3. know	5. ...want	6. yard
6. for	1. good	3. the	6. ...are	3. a	2. dough!
3. we	5. to	4. idea!	3. hurry —	4. ...need	5. better!

---

1. Top Card Playing Company
"Come see us when you...

2. B&B Baking and Loan
"Come see us when you...

3. Al's Barber Shop
"Come see us when you...

4. Larry's Lightbulbs
"Come see us when you...

5. Elegant Eyewear
"Come see us when you...

6. Good Deal Real Estate
"Come see us when you...

Why was the King of Hearts so upset?
Because his Ace was in the hole.

What do you call it when 5 royal cards get together?
A full house.

When the scientist didn't like Frankenstein's attitude, what did he do about it?
He "changed" his mind.

Why was the garbage man so sad?
He was down in the dumps.

Why was the cowboy so tired?
Because his giddy-up-and-go gotty-up-and-went!

What do you get when you drop a 500-pound potato off the top of a skyscraper?
500 pounds of s-mashed potatoes.

What do you call a really cold puppy?
A chili dog.

If **Lilly** licks a lollipop while watching 3 30-minute cartoons and she only **licks** halfway through her **lolly**, how long will it take to finish it?

90 more minutes

Clarence the **clown** took off his big shoes, curly wig, baggy pants, polka-dotted tie, all of his makeup, suspenders, and his gloves. On the way to his trailer, a little **girl** stopped to say, "You're a clown, aren't you?" **How did she know?**

He forgot to take off his red nose!

Some days **Jack** felt really **up**, and some days Jack felt really **down**. **Why?**

He's a Jack-in-the-box

Who am I?

I liked to make people laugh and I would use anything I could think of—songs, poems, stories, art, and cartoons. I wrote several fun and silly books for children, like *Where the Sidewalk Ends*. **Who am I?**

Shel Silverstein

Words to Know

memory:

Ability to store information in your brain. Without your memory, you could never remember your brother's birthday or where you put your favorite book. And did you know that memory is one of the things required for laughter?

What type of print will you never find in a newspaper?

A footprint.

What can adult teeth have?

Baby teeth.

How do clouds make other clouds get out of their way?

They use their foghorns.

How can you tie something so you will always remember it?

With a "forget-me knot."

What did one "Most Wanted" poster say to the other?

I've been framed!

Every once in a while, the workers at the **perfume** factory smell a horrible, strong **skunk** smell. **Why is this?**

Some perfumes are made from the smelly spray that comes from skunks

What object can go up and come down all by itself?

A helium balloon—when you blow it up it goes up, but in a few days it comes back down

What two things combine to look like a miniature tornado?

A bathtub drain and water

What's So Funny?

Jordan has some very silly dreams. One night he dreamt that he was a clown and when he woke up his nose *was* a little red. The next time he dreamed he was a king, only to find when he woke up that his comforter was around him like a robe. But tonight's dream had to be the silliest of all! Jordan dreamt he was sleepwalking! **What's so funny?**

When he woke up he was in the yard!

Chapter 6

Crossing Over

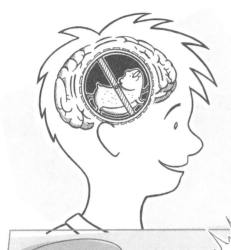

Fun Fact

Use Your Head!
Everyone has a *pons* (meaning "bridge"). Your pons is a part of your brain that is in charge of many things, like sorting all of the information you take in to decide what is important enough to think about.

When **Geoffrey** wrote a paper about crossing the English Channel for English class, he left out the **crossing** part. Because of this, no one could read his paper. **Why?**

He didn't cross his t's

How can 6 **toothpicks** have only 6 **points?**

When you make 2 triangles out of them

Do you know how to get a riddle really upset?
Take away its d's and you'll "rile" it.

What do you get when you cross 40 robbers with a herd of sheep?
Ali Baa Baa and 40 thieves.

Why did the math teacher cross the road?
Because he had "2."

Who wrote the book 1001 Crosswords?
Chris Cross.

What do you get if you cross a movie theater with a palm reader?
Show-'n'-tell.

Why did the playground cross the road?
To get to the other slide.

Who am I?

I was a powerful Egyptian queen, known for my beauty, intelligence, and power. Unfortunately, it all came to an end because of a Roman general. **Who am I?**
Cleopatra

When **Maggie** and **Annette** found 2 nails on the ground, one **lying** across the other, Maggie bet Annette she couldn't get them apart without **touching** them. Maggie lost the bet. How did Annette manage to do the **trick?**

She used 2 magnets

If a train going **40 miles** an hour reaches a railroad crossing in **40 minutes**, how long will it take a train going **20 miles** an hour to reach it?

80 minutes

What's So Funny?

Sam was very superstitious. He never walked under ladders or went anywhere on Friday the 13th, and he always carried his lucky penny everywhere he went. All in all, his plan worked very well—until one day everything went wrong. "This just can't be possible," Sam thought. **What's so funny?**

He hadn't noticed that a black cat had crossed his path!

Cross Plumber

Cross out the letters that appear more than three times in the letter grid. Collect the remaining letters from left to right and top to bottom, and write them in order on the blank lines. When you are finished, you will discover the answer to this riddle:

What do you get when you cross a plumber with a jeweler?

_ _ _ _ _

_ _ _ _ _ _ _ _

_ _ _ _ _ _ _ !

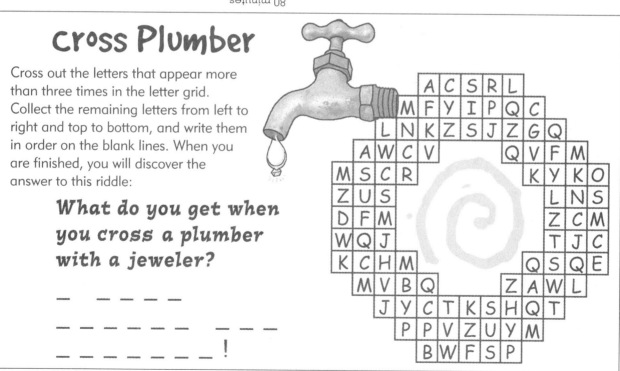

Why Did the Lion...

As you find your way through the maze from START to END, collect the letters.
When you read them in order, you will discover the answer to this riddle:

Why did the lion cross the grassland?

Words to Know

ESP:

Extrasensory perception is the believed ability to have a type of sixth sense. Someone who claims to be able to read your mind or know your thoughts is said to have ESP.

What do you get when you cross a snowman with a pickup full of carrots?
Frozen food in a delivery truck!

What do you get when you cross an automobile with music?
Cartoons (car tunes).

What time is it when you cross an alarm clock with a skunk?
Time to go!

Why did the cheater have 2 X's on his head?
He had been double-crossed.

Why did the fish cross the road?
Because he was already "caught" in the middle.

Why did the fertilizer cross the road?
Because the grass wasn't greener on the other side!

As **Cami** began crossing the railroad tracks, she realized a **train** would be there soon. She saw no train, heard no sound, but knew it just the same. **How did she know?**

She could feel the vibration on the tracks

As **Rhonda** saw the "walk" sign light up, she started to cross the **street**. Instantly, several cars screeched to a halt inches from her. **Why?**

She was looking at the sign for the other direction

Try This Try This Try This

Testing for ESP
Do you or someone you know have ESP? One test for ESP that you can try on your friends is to make a few cards with circles, wavy lines, or dots on them. After you have shown them the cards, look at one of the cards and ask your friend to sense which one you are looking at. You can take turns testing each other to see who does best.

Why wouldn't the first skeleton cross the road?
No guts!

Why did the second skeleton cross it?
No brains!

And why didn't the third skeleton cross it?
He just didn't have the heart to!

Why wouldn't the rooster cross the road?
He was too much of a chicken.

Where does an X always sit?
In the cross section.

Why did the bee cross the road?
He wanted to see his "honey."

In science class, **Amanda** learned that when you put salt on a **slug**, something very horrible happens. **Do you know what?**

The slug melts

When **Lila** told her mother she would come straight home after **school**, her mother knew it wasn't true. **How?**

She saw that Lila's fingers were crossed

"I **spin**, yet I am never dizzy.
I have clouds, but have no **rain**.
As I cross the **land**, you cannot see how deadly I am."
What is it?

A dust storm

Fun Fact

A Riddle of a Name
"Rumpelstiltskin" is a well-known fairy tale, maybe because it was part of the famed Brothers Grimm collection of fairy tales. In the tale, Rumpelstiltskin tells the Queen that she has to guess his name, or he will take her firstborn child. Do you remember how the Queen solved this riddle?

Hinky Pinkies

The answer to each Hinky Pinky riddle is two rhyming words of two syllables each. Write the answers into the numbered grid.

EXTRA FUN: When you're finished, read down the shaded column to find the answer to one more Hinky Pinky:

What do you get when you cross a monster with someone who works at your school?

What do you get when you cross…

1. …a sticky candy with a hot breakfast drink?
2. …a comic book action hero with a detective?
3. …a lawyer with a large bird of prey?
4. …a South American pack animal with a serious play?
5. …a baby cat with a winter handwarmer?
6. …a comedian with a rabbit?
7. …a werewolf with Tinkerbell?
8. …a molecule with a violin?
9. …a tired person with a pointy tent?
10. …a king with a small hunting dog?
11. …a mad scientist with a white and yellow flower?
12. …a large tropical bird with an orange vegetable?
13. …a hot pepper with a boy named William?
14. …a field of daisies with a generator?
15. …a reptile with a magical man?

#	Grid letters (with shaded column)
1.	F F ... F F
2.	E R ... E R
3.	G ... G
4.	A M ... A M
5.	T T ... T T
6.	U ... U
7.	A I ... A I
8.	I ... L ... I ... L
9.	Y ... E E
10.	R E ... B E
11.	Y ... Y
12.	R R ... R R
13.	... I ... Y
14.	O W ... O W
15.	A D ... A D

Which pair of the following **words**, crossed exactly in the middle like a **crossword**, will join at the same **letter?** Party, money, stand, brunt, flash, salad.

Stand and flash

Crossing what two things creates a lot of **foam** and so may be used to simulate a **volcano?**

Baking soda and vinegar

Mr. Wilson pulls up to a pedestrian crossing, but no one is there. Can he go on? The answer is no! **Why?** Hint: Is there something else that is stopping him?

Yes—the light is still red

Fun Fact

Crazy Talk
Did you know that between your left brain and your right brain you have a corpus callosum that allows the two sides of your brain to "talk"? The corpus callosum lets you hear something on one side of your brain and then picture it with the other side.

Who am I?

I had a theory or idea that man may have started out as a chimpanzee or ape and then slowly changed or evolved into what he is today. **Who am I?**

Charles Darwin

Why did the Martians keep bringing more men?
They needed "Xtra terrestrials."

Why did the bank teller cross the road?
He didn't have any cents.

Why did the rhino swim to the other side of the river?
He wanted to get his "point" across.

Why did the squirrel cross the busy road?
I guess we'll never know!

What did the Troll warn the Three Billy Goats Gruff?
Don't cross me!

Why did the electrician light up?
His wires were crossed.

What do you get when you cross an ape with a magician?

Hairy Houdini (Harry Houdini).

How did George Washington and Huck Finn cross the river?

George chopped down the cherry tree and Huck made a raft out of it.

Why did the owl cross the road?

Whooooo cares?

Why did the book cross the road?

It was looking for cover.

How did the pharmacist get all of his medicine across the road?

He "drug" it.

Why did the nail cross the road?

He was bent on it.

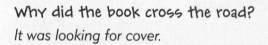

rebus:

Words to Know

A kind of puzzle in which a picture represents a word or part of a word. Sometimes a rebus will be used in a storybook to introduce new words, or in a game to challenge the guesser to solve the picture puzzle.

Try This **Try This** **Try This** **Try This**

Tell a Story in Pictures

You can make a rebus of your own by writing a short story or retelling a familiar one using pictures that you draw in the place of some of the words. An example could be the story of Goldilocks and the Three Bears. You could substitute a picture of a bear each time the word "bear" appears.

What is a **cross** between *star* and *led*?

Star-t-led

How did **Peter** get across the Nottafoot River without a **boat?**

He walked—it was only 11 inches deep

When **Xavier** would turn in his homework, his **teacher** knew which paper was his, even though he always forgot to sign his name. **How did she know?**

He always did the Xtra credit

What do angry quilters make?
Cross stitches.

Why did the rope cross the road?
Why "knot"?

Why didn't the crossword get the answer?
He was too puzzled!

What can you find at the intersections in church?
Look for "cross" walks.

Why did the letters cross the road?
It was EZ.

How do roads talk?
They use "sign" language.

Who am I?

I grew up in Pennsylvania telling funny stories and making people laugh. My big break came when I told a few jokes on TV. I am a very well-known comedian and had a family TV show named after me.
Who am I?

Bill Cosby

When the **water** ran across the floor of the pool house, no one panicked. **Why?**

They were hosing off the floor

When the **plane** crossed the sky at a weird angle, the control tower knew there was trouble and called for help. The plane's **radio** was out and the pilot was too far away to signal. How did the tower learn of the **problem?**

The pilot was a sky writer

Words to Know

comedy:

A type of amusement that relies on humor to entertain people. Funny stories and actions are often used in a comedy routine.

Otto was really confused when he received a letter from his eye **doctor** that read: "Tsn't tt about ttme you came tn for a vtstt?" **What was wrong?**

Otto's i's were crossed because he was cross-eyed!

Chapter 7

Perfectly at Home

Katherine's room is too far away from the bathroom to hear whether someone is using the **shower**. And yet, Katherine knew that her mom had taken a shower this morning. **What tipped her off?**

The shower was still wet

What do the **words** "end," "multiplication," "kitchen," and "coffee" have in common? **Hint:** They are all adjectives for one noun.

They are all a kind of table

Daniel filled a bathtub up to 1 inch from the top. No more **water** was put in it, but it still overflowed. **How can that be?**

He got in

Who am I?

You may have laughed at the troubles of poor old Charlie Brown, a cartoon character I created. I drew and wrote about Charlie and all the rest of the "Peanuts" gang to make others laugh. **Who am I?**

Charles Schulz

Words to Know

teasing:

Teasing is bothering, annoying, or taunting others by making fun of them. Some teasing is just for fun—nothing to get offended about—but sometimes teasing becomes mean and should be stopped.

Why did the poltergeist try to scare the gambler out of his house?
I don't know, but he didn't have a ghost of a chance.

What do builders write on?
Construction paper.

Why did the actor get fired?
Because he brought the house down.

What did the old block name his son?
Chip.

Why did the plug-in have to stay home?
She was grounded.

Why did the cow and the moon have to eat out all the time?
Because their dishes ran away with their spoons!

Why did the hammer get into trouble?
Because he hit the nail on the head!

Where do roses sleep?
In a flower bed.

How did the window know which bugs were good?
She screened them.

How many sides does a house have?
Two—an "in" side and an "out" side.

What kind of dance did the porch learn?
The two-step.

Why did the bee have to stay home?
It had hives.

Tommy's Tennis Tongue Twister
Try this tongue twister: Tommy tied 20 tiny tennis shoes. After you say that 5 times fast, how about making up a few of your own to try on your family and friends? Here's a hint to making new tongue twister— pick a consonant (in the case of this tongue twister, it's "t") and then try to come up with a bunch of words with that consonant.

Color Me In!

Fun Fact

Twist and Shout!
Tongue twisters have been entertaining people—tying up their tongues—for years. Many tongue twisters have made their way into children's books and collections. A good tongue twister is almost impossible to say quickly.

What's So Funny?

One day, while Goldilocks was on her way to the Three Bears' house, she got distracted. Eventually, she remembered where she was going and arrived at the cottage in the woods, just as the bears were leaving for their walk. As Goldie opened the door, she gasped! **What's so funny?**

The bears had already eaten!

"The **longer** it goes, the **shorter** it grows." What is it?

A burning candle

Bob and **Bill** decided to build a tree house. They've got a tree with a trunk that's **15 feet** tall, so they decided to build stairs that go up the tree. Unfortunately, all they have are **6 boards**. How far apart do Bob and Bill need to nail the **6 boards** so that the stairs are evenly spread out?

2.5 feet from the center of each board

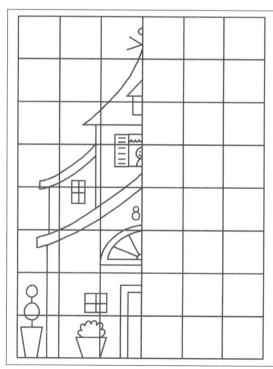

Half a House?

Seems like the builder only finished half of this very fancy house. Can you complete the job? Draw the other half of the house, copying the first half square by square.

Next, figure out what letter goes in each box, below. When you are finished, you will get the answer to this riddle:

What kind of house does every house builder know how to build?

C-2	H+6	J-5	Z-3	K+4	S-5	B+3

Dream, Dream, Dream

You can try to figure out what you or someone else's dreams might mean. If you look in a dream encyclopedia or dream interpretation book, you will see what some people believe are the meanings or clues behind the things you may dream about—for example, falling can symbolize a loss. Of course, in order to interpret your dreams, you first have to try to remember them when you wake up.

Bathtub, toilet, shower—what's **missing** from this group?

Sink

As **Barry's** mom walked through the house she saw a bag of **candy** in the entryway and a wrapper in the dining room. By the time she reached the **kitchen**, she knew Barry didn't like the candy very much. **How did she know?**

He had spit the candy out in the trashcan

Why did it take the ant so long to get home?
It was "uphill" all the way.

What do pans like to eat?
Pot pies.

Why didn't the china hutch like to be teased?
He could "dish" it out, but he couldn't take it.

What state covers more ground than any other?
Floor-ida!

Why did General Custer sit in his chair all the time?
Because he had made his last stand.

Why did the chicken run out of the house screaming?
It couldn't take being "coop-ed" up in the house!

Marissa is writing a school report on her computer at home. The other night, a **virus** invaded her computer and her report got all jumbled. Can you tell what this **sentence** was and what the report was about? **Here is the sentence:** Sometimesth eyli keto eatho lesincl othing,es peciallyth ingsma deofwo ol.

The sentence is, "Sometimes they like to eat holes in clothing, especially things made of wool." The report was about moths.

What did the windows do when they saw the storm coming?

They shuttered!

What did all the king's horses and all the king's men say when Humpty Dumpty fell off the wall?

He was a good egg!

What do 24 hours do at night?

Call it a day.

Why couldn't the chair be fixed?

It would cost an arm and a leg.

How did the tools get the truth out of the wood?

They drilled it.

Why didn't the window have any money?

It was broke.

Mr. Axeman the carpenter asked his assistant **Woody** if he knew the three things that make a pen different from a pencil. **Do you know?**

The three things are the letters "c," "i," and "l."

Who am I?

I wear a striped shirt and big glasses, and I'm a part of many puzzle books. You can try to find me in pictures, where I may be skiing on a mountain full of people or hiding out in a gigantic shopping mall. **Who am I?**

Waldo from Where's Waldo?

Which Window?

Roberto lives in a big, old house that has been turned into a bunch of apartments. Use the clues below to figure out which window is his.

- **The window to the right of Roberto's has a plant on the windowsill.**
- **The window above Roberto's has no shade.**

- Roberto's window has **curtains that his mom made for him.**
- Roberto's window **does not have a shutter.**

EXTRA FUN: Read the letters in the windows from bottom to top, and right to left, and you will find the answer to this riddle:

Which side of a house gets the most rain?

fun House

Can you find 24 funny things in this living room? When you're finished,
see if you can figure out what's so funny about the answer to this riddle:

What kind of house weighs the least?
A LIGHTHOUSE!

Fun Fact

Ego Mania

Did you know you have an "ego"?
Your ego is your "self." Many believe it is
the main force behind your personality—it's who
you really are.

How do you make a **house** using only **6 nails?**

Take 4 nails and lay them out in a square, head to point; then put the other 2 on top of the square to make the triangle roof.

When **Breanna** went to **Brittney's** house, she had planned to be there for breakfast and lunch. To make things simpler they had **brunch**. What did they end up missing?

E, a, k, f, a, s, t, and l

When an **ice sculptor** left his house on Wednesday, he had **4** beautiful swans in the freezer. Yet when he returned on Sunday, **they were gone!** No one broke in and there is a logical answer. What could have happened?

He left the freezer door open

How does Rover stay out of the doghouse?

He buries the evidence.

What do bathrooms in outer space have?

Meteor showers.

Why did the porch tell the steps to knock it off?

They kept "stair-ing"!

What do homes wear when it gets cold out?

House coats.

What does every floor of the house have to have before bed?

Bedtime stories.

What do you call a hat that follows you everywhere you go?

A stalking cap!

Why didn't the outside of the house understand what was so funny?

It was an "inside" joke.

What did the swingset say to the sandbox when the teeter-totter arrived?

Wow! Did you SEE what I SAW?

How can you tell when a toilet's not well?

It's flushed.

What's an envelope's favorite part of the house?

The "seal-ing."

Why did the colander have to go to the doctor?

It was a little strained!

Why couldn't the ball player ever go home?

He was out in "left" field.

Who am I?

I invented a test that used 10 different inkblots. These images helped psychologists try to understand how a patient thinks by what the person felt he or she was seeing in the blots. **Who am I?**

Hermann Rorschach

Mrs. Smith lives in a 20-story apartment building. She lives on the **15th** floor, and yet she never passes by the **13th** floor. What's the explanation?

Because 13 is thought to be an unlucky number, some apartment buildings don't have a 13th floor

Jasmine's dining room table has enough room for only **6** people, yet every night **8** eat there. **How can that be?**

There are 6 human family members plus the dog and the cat—they eat under the table

One night **2 burglars** broke into the Joneses' house. As soon as they were inside, they heard a **voice**. The burglars got scared and left. No one was home, **so whom did they hear?**

The announcer on the radio, which Sally Jones had forgotten to turn off

Words to Know

dream:

A group of thoughts, images, and feelings that you experience during the REM (rapid eye movement) portion of your sleep. Another type of dreaming is daydreaming—imagining something while you are awake.

Every time **Clarence** went into the house, something went wrong, very wrong. Clarence would **gain** weight only to instantly **lose** it again. Once he even swore he was shrinking. But the next day he felt taller than ever. **Why?**

Clarence went to a fun house with distorting mirrors

Liza lives in a grey house, while **Lisa** lives in a house that's gray. **What's the difference?**

The spelling of "grey" and "gray"

Inkblot Tests

To create your own inkblot guessing game or test, you will need 10 blots. To make them, all you need are 10 pieces of paper folded once and then opened. Pour a little bit of paint on one side of the paper. Then, refold the paper, pressing gently on the blot. Open the paper again and let the paint dry. Now all you need is someone to test. Start by asking, "When you look at this picture, what do you see?"

How did the tools get from the house to the tool store?

The compass gave directions, while the screwdriver drove.

When the princess arrived at the castle and found the new labyrinth, how did she feel?

A maze-d!

What does Sir Galahad turn on when he gets scared at night?

A knight light.

In **Centerville**, it normally takes **2 days** to send a letter from one house to another—**1 day** to mail it, and **1** to have it delivered. But Mrs. Smith always receives her mail the same day it is sent. **How can that be?**

She married the postman!

How could the **carpenter** know how tall to make his door just by using his **hands?**

He could cut the door according to his arm span, because your arm span is the same as your height

73

Write your own jokes here:

_____

_____

_____

_____

_____

_____

_____

_____

_____

_____

_____

_____

_____

Chapter 8
Let's Play Sports

What's So Funny?

Keep Pedaling!

Lance Pedlin is a famous biker who can pedal for hours on his bike. One day, he got on and started pedaling, and he kept going and going, but when he was done, he was still where he started. **What's so funny?**

He was on his exercise bike

What happens when a clumsy football player plays ball?

A field trip.

Why did the racecar driver jump into the pool?

He wanted to put in a few laps.

Why did the golfer have to buy new shoes?

He had a "hole in one."

What did the high diver wear to his wedding?

A "swim" suit.

What does Dracula take with him when he goes to a ball game?

His bat.

What do dolphins wear to the beach?

Swim fins.

Words to Know

sense:

The ability to see, smell, hear, touch, and taste all of the things that you come in contact with are made possible by your 5 senses. Your brain relies on the senses to perceive the outside world.

Try This Try This Try This

It's Not Funny to Me!

No two people have exactly the same sense of humor. If you want to see this for yourself, you can conduct a little experiment. Find yourself 5 jokes and 5 volunteers. Read each joke separately to your volunteers, then write down who laughed at which ones. When you are done, you can chart your results and compare them. What did you discover?

If there are **9** players on a **baseball** team and **11** players on a **football** team, how many **swimmers** are there on the swim team?

Any number—swim teams vary in number of teammates.

The **mountain** climbers had almost reached the top of the cliff when their rope began to fray. For each inch they moved, **2** strands would break. The climbers had **49** inches to go, with a **100**-ply rope. **Will they make it?**

Yes

When is **8** not twice as much as **4**?

When you're trying on shoes

Amanda is an excellent swimmer. She can hold her breath for **2** minutes. She can also swim **300** yards in half an hour. So, can Amanda swim **25** yards without coming up for air?

No, she would only be able to go 20 yards

What did one twine say to the other right before he fell into a hole?
JUMP, ROPE!

Why did the tennis players get into so much trouble?
They were making a lot of "racket."

Where do basketball players settle their arguments?
In "court."

How do swimmers get where they are going?
In car "pools."

What sport did Little Red Riding Hood play best?
"Basket" ball.

What sport is after "nine"?
Ten-nis.

Night Games

Start with the number 1 and connect all the dots in order.

Which animals are always invited to night baseball games?

What sports item hangs upside down from its toes?

A baseball "bat."

What sport makes a lot of people "jumpy"?

Trampolining.

What is a baseball player's favorite part of the playground?

The slide.

What do catchers wear when it gets cold out?

Their gloves.

What did the photographer say to the badminton rackets?

Watch the birdie!

What kind of shoes do woodpeckers dance in?

Tap shoes.

Who am I?

I am the one who helped "Little Red" solve the riddle of my identity, by showing her what big teeth I have. **Who am I?**

The Wolf

Fun Fact

Calling Your Conscience
Did you know that there is a part of you that is very aware of what is going on around you all the time? It is called your conscience. Your conscious mind remembers and can recall different things that have happened to you.

If the pitching machine at **Sports World** shoots out **1** ball every **10** seconds while you are trying to hit it, how long will it take to empty the machine of its **90** balls?

15 minutes

John works in sports every day, yet he never goes home sore or tired or sweaty. **How can this be?**

He's the scorekeeper.

Do you see a **pattern** here? Number of **catchers** on a baseball team, number of **teams** in a game, number of **strikes** before an out, number of **bases** in a diamond.

1, 2, 3, 4

Where do bad gymnasts go?
Behind parallel bars!

How did the archer get to the contest?
He followed the arrows.

Why do athletes need so much money?
Because of the "tro-fees."

How do monarchs swim?
They do the butterfly stroke.

What is a washing machine's favorite pastime?
Cycling.

What did the desperate golfer eat?
His sand-wedge.

Overcoming Any Obstacle
Have you ever made a silly object obstacle course? You and your friends will have fun trying to see who can complete the course the fastest. Your course can include writing the first letter of your name in a plate of whipped cream, walking 20 steps with a tennis ball between your knees, and popping a balloon by sitting on it, as well as any other silly things you can think of. And the winner of the silly course gets a silly prize!

When **Eve** ran in track she was covered in sweat, yet by the time she was ready to go **home**, her skin was dry. **Why?**

The sweat evaporated

When the school **rowing team** left the dock, they paddled for **15** minutes, then turned around. **Ten** minutes later they returned. How come it took them **5** minutes less to come back?

The wind was against them going out and with them coming back

hoops!

Fill in the answers to the clues, putting one letter in each numbered space. Then transfer the letters to the boxes that have the same numbers. When all the boxes are filled in correctly, you will have the answer to the riddle!

A. __ __ __   Easily frighened; timid
   10 2 7

B. __ __ __ __ __   Woman on her wedding day
   20 9 19 17 3

C. __ __ __   What a spider builds
   13 8 21

D. __ __ __ __ __   One thickness of something
   5 11 15 23 18

E. __ __   Short nickname for father
   4 14

F. __ __ __ __ __   Place in a barn for a horse
   16 1 6 12 22

Why is a basketball court often wet?

1	2	3		4	5	6	7	8	9	10

11	12	13	14	15	16		17	18	19	20	21	22	23	!

When **Tina** the tennis pro returned all of the balls that came to her, none came back to her. **Why?**

She wasn't playing with another person—she was using a ball machine

When **Skip** brought his new track shoes home, he realized the store clerk had put the wrong **laces** in the box. These laces were only half as long as they needed to be. **What did Skip do?**

He skipped every other hole when he laced them

Which one of these **does not** belong? Helmet, goalie, touchdown, quarterback.

Goalie—the rest relate to football

Who am I?

Most people know me for my experiments with a dog and a bell. I trained my dog to be hungry each time I rang the bell. I liked to study the brain and people's reflexes. **Who am I?**

Ivan Pavlov

Fun Fact

Underneath the Conscious

Your conscious mind is composed of all that you remember and have knowledge of. But there is another part of your mind, called your subconscious. The subconscious may store information without your remembering it.

When **Kyle** fell out of the boat, everyone waited for his return. After **20** minutes, he still did not come up for air. **Why?**

He was scuba diving

"I dive but use no **water**,
I **fly** but have no wings,
I land but have no **wheels**."
Who is it?

A skydiver

Balls of Fun

There are many sports that have their own special ball to use. Can you unscramble the names of ten of these sports? When you're finished, find your way through the maze of balls!

EXTRA FUN: Can you think of 10 more sports that use balls?

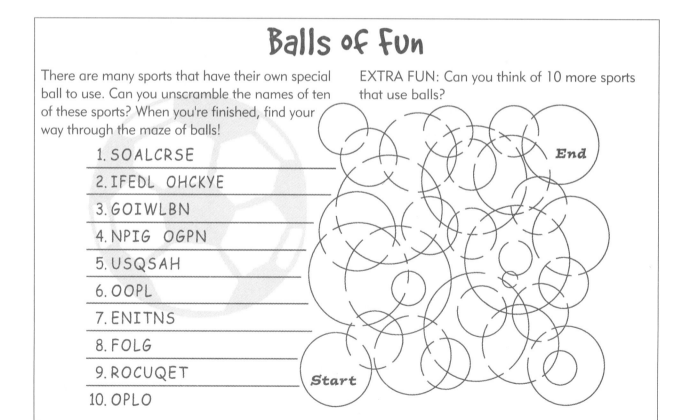

1. SOALCRSE _____
2. IFEDL OHCKYE _____
3. GOIWLBN _____
4. NPIG OGPN _____
5. USQSAH _____
6. OOPL _____
7. ENITNS _____
8. FOLG _____
9. ROCUQET _____
10. OPLO _____

Start

End

What do these **words** have in **common?**
Hole, hazard, slice, wood.

They are all golf terms

What do these **things** have in **common?**
Diamond, slide, innings, umpire.

They are all baseball terms

In what **sport** are you doing better as
your score is getting **lower?**

Golf

Try This Try This Try This

Test Your Reading Skills
You know how to read, but can you read
upside down? Don't worry, you don't
have to be *hanging*
upside down. Just flip the
book upside down and see
if you can keep reading. Is it
easy or difficult? As you may
discover, it's not easy! But, who
knows, you may actually be able
to read faster upside down than
right side up!

**Words
to
Know**

IQ:
IQ or Intelligence Quotient is a measure of
one's ability to think. An IQ test allows
people to measure genius as well as
normal thinking ability.

**What did the mountain
climber tell her stinky
boots to do?**
Take a hike!

**Where do all the sports
shirts come from?**
Jersey.

**What did the hockey player ask the
puck right before the game?**
Want to "stick" around for a while?

Why don't rockets play football?
They prefer liftoffs to touchdowns.

What is a dish's favorite pastime?
"Bowl-ing."

What did one sports shoe say to the other?
Nothing, they were tongue-tied.

What comes after a ball?
B ball.

What do baby basketballs do?
Dribble.

What sport hurts the most?
Paddleball.

What was Jack and Jill's best sporting event?
Downhill racing.

Where do 4 woods hang out?
At a golf "club."

What is a fly swatter's favorite sport?
Squash.

First base ball game day. What should come **next?**

Day off. First base, baseball, ball game, game day, day off!

"I have a **tongue**, but cannot speak.
I have a **toe**, but have no feet."
What is it?

A shoe

Who am I?

When Belle tried to solve the mystery of her missing father, she found a new mystery in me. She was a beauty, and she transformed me into a beautiful person as well. **Who am I?**

The Beast from Beauty and the Beast

Chapter 9
All in the Family

A Matter of Symmetry

Being symmetrical means that your right side and left side are mirror images of each other. The human body is symmetrical because we have 2 eyes, 2 arms, and 2 legs, and they are very much alike. But do they act the same? For example, most people have one hand that they prefer writing with. But what if you tried writing with a hand you don't normally use? If you can do most things with both hands, you are what they call "ambidextrous."

If **two** twins were both to **marry** and they both had twins, and then their **twins** had twins, **how many** twins would there be?

14 twins

Every year **Dillon** gets older, he gets a dollar more for his birthday. How much **money** will he have when he is **10?**

$55

What type of father has no sole?
The barefoot type.

What did Samuel Wilson become when he married an aunt?
Uncle Sam.

If you can't tell your Grandpa something, what do you do?
Telegram (tell a Gram)!

Which one of Mother Earth's children warms her heart the most?
Her "sun"!

What did the Old Woman Who Lived in a Shoe need more than anything else?
A break!

What does your mother's sister become when she's nervous?
Aunt-sy.

Words to Know

humor:

Something that is designed to be comical or amusing. Jokes and comedy are said to be humorous, because they can make us laugh.

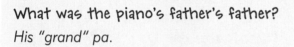

Who am I?

It was my job to solve the riddle of the missing girl who lost her glass slipper. The only way to solve the problem was to try the shoe on every foot in the kingdom. **Who am I?**

The Prince from Cinderella

What was the piano's father's father?
His "grand" pa.

What do you call it when your sister demands to enter?
In-Sis-ting.

Who takes care of baby moths?
Their moth-er.

Where do apples search for their roots?
In their family tree.

What does a little doe call her mother?
Mommy deer.

What do you call a ladder's kid?
Its step child.

Let's say that in the **Wilkins family**, X = red hair, and Y = brown hair, and Z = blonde hair. If there are **2 times more** X's than Y's or Z's, what are the odds of the **fifth** child having **blonde** hair?

1 in 4

Fun Fact

Just What the Doctor Ordered
Some say laughter is the best medicine, and that may very well be true. Without laughter or happiness you may become sad or depressed. To snap out of it, it's possible that all you need is a good laugh.

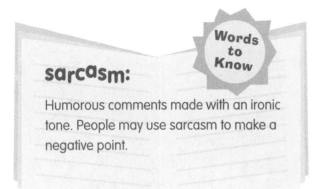

Words to Know

sarcasm:

Humorous comments made with an ironic tone. People may use sarcasm to make a negative point.

Identical twins **Cindy** and **Wendy** took a long walk in the forest. After a while they decided to play **hide and seek**. Cindy quickly found Wendy . . . or so she thought. Soon, it turned out that Cindy had actually found *herself*. **How could this be?**

She saw her own reflection in the water

What is a family of kittens after they are 13 days old?

2 weeks old.

Why was Old Mother Hubbard so scared of her cupboards?

They were "bear."

What did Peter Peter Pumpkin Eater's wife sell?

Shells by the seashore.

What did King Tut call his mother?

Mummy.

Who had the angriest child in history?

Dolly Madison ("mad is son").

What is small, buzzes, and lives by the water?

Bay bees (babies).

When **David** called a family of **ducks** over to feed them, his voiced echoed throughout the **hills**. But when the ducks called back, David only heard one reply. **Why?**

A duck's quack doesn't echo

What's So Funny?

One day, Wendy told her mother that she wasn't sure why, but it seemed like suddenly her whole world had turned upside down. Everyone was frowning and nothing was as it was supposed to be. Not even gravity. **What's so funny?**

She was standing on her head

Who were the Wrong Sisters' siblings?
The Wright Brothers.

How many kids did Daniel's uncle have?
None, his aunt had all of them.

How did the baby cabbage know he was winning?
He was a "head" of the game.

What kind of family reunions do puzzles have?
They gave "get (it) togethers."

What did the fishing poles always wish for?
A "reel" family.

What do track stars call their family members?
Relay-tions.

Who am I?

As a cartoonist and movie producer, I wanted to share my "world" with you. I hope that you could see it wasn't such a small world, after all. Someday you may "land" at one of my amusement parks.
Who am I?

Walt Disney

Big Brothers

Mr. and Mrs. Wood have a large family. They have always been married to each other, and neither one has any children with anyone else. How is it possible, then, that one child in the Wood family has four brothers, while another child in the Wood family has five brothers?

The answer to this brain teaser is hidden in the letter grid. Use these clues to help figure it out:

• **The answer starts in one of the four corners.**
• **You read the answer in logical order, one word after the other.**
• **You must add the punctuation.**

D	L	I	H	C	X	I	S	E
R	O	B	E	H	T	F	O	V
E	Y	L	I	H	W	S	E	A
N	S	E	I	F	E	R	N	H
F	W	T	V	S	V	E	O	S
I	I	H	E	R	A	H	Y	D
V	L	E	B	E	H	T	N	O
E	L	G	R	H	L	O	A	O
B	H	I	O	T	L	R	L	W
O	A	R	L	W	I	B	R	E
Y	V	E	F	O	U	R	I	H
S	A	N	D	O	N	E	G	T

89

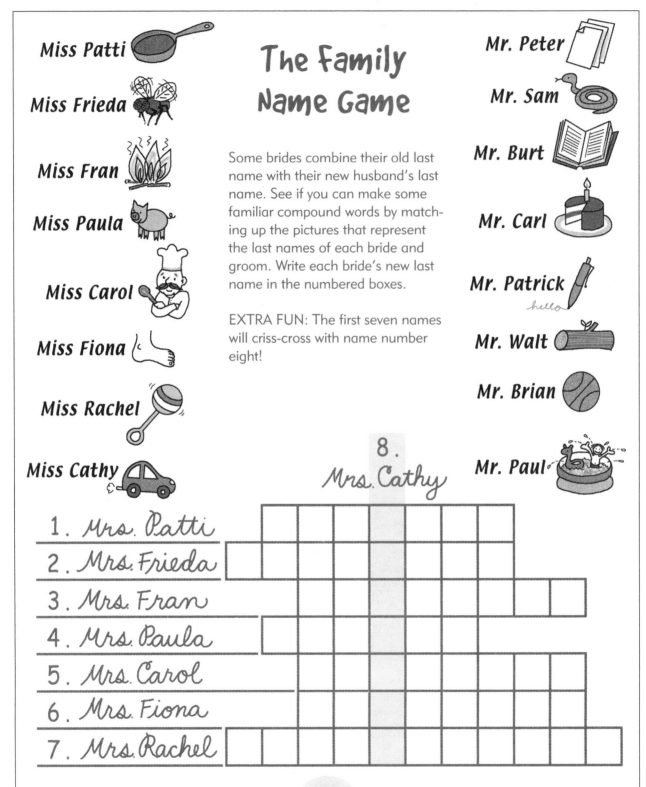

The Family Name Game

Miss Patti

Miss Frieda

Miss Fran

Miss Paula

Miss Carol

Miss Fiona

Miss Rachel

Miss Cathy

Mr. Peter

Mr. Sam

Mr. Burt

Mr. Carl

Mr. Patrick

Mr. Walt

Mr. Brian

Mr. Paul

Some brides combine their old last name with their new husband's last name. See if you can make some familiar compound words by matching up the pictures that represent the last names of each bride and groom. Write each bride's new last name in the numbered boxes.

EXTRA FUN: The first seven names will criss-cross with name number eight!

8.
Mrs. Cathy

1. Mrs. Patti

2. Mrs. Frieda

3. Mrs. Fran

4. Mrs. Paula

5. Mrs. Carol

6. Mrs. Fiona

7. Mrs. Rachel

90

What were the Three Little Kittens who lost their mittens?
Cold.

What do suits have that no one else can have?
Family ties.

Why wouldn't Jack in the Beanstalk's mother let him watch football?
Because of the Giants.

Whom did the bug's uncle marry?
His "ant."

Why did they take Tina's cousin away 2 times?
Because he was twice removed.

What was the shredder's distant grandmother called?
Grate, grate, grate grandmother.

If 3 **sisters** have 3 **daughters** each, and each of their daughters has 3 daughters, how many **females** are in their family?

39 females

While **Cassie** and her mother were shopping, her mother asked if Cassie would bring her a **pair**. "A pair of what?" asked Cassie. "Just one pair," answered her mom. **What did she mean?**

She wanted a pear!

Amazing Mazes
Here's a fun trick to try while solving a maze puzzle. Take the paper with the maze and place it horizontally over a hard surface next to a vertical mirror. Now, can you get through the maze by looking at the mirror? Remember: You can't look at the maze itself—just at its reflection in the mirror.

91

Watch out!

The letters in each column go in the squares directly below them, but not in the same order. Black squares are the spaces between words. When you have correctly filled in the grid, you will have a silly conversation between a worried mom and her daughter!

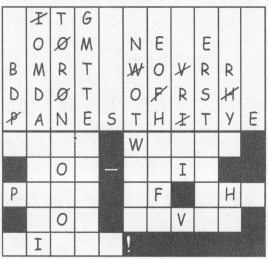

There are **11 children** in Mary's family. If there are **3** more **girls** than **boys**, how many boys and girls are there?

7 girls and 4 boys

How long will it take for the Tillman Triplets to eat **3 ice cream** cones, if it takes the Thompson Twins **10** minutes to eat **2**?

10 minutes, assuming they eat at the same speed

Why did the mother dollar take so many pictures of her "new" dollar?
She knew someday soon he would "change."

What do mother boots have?
Baby booties.

Who can go the longer distance, your mom or your dad?
Your "farther."

How long did it take the drills to have their baby?
Just a little "bit."

Why did Mr. and Mrs. Trampoline take their son to see the doctor?
He seemed a little "jumpy."

Fun Fact

A Running Maze

Human-sized mazes are known as labyrinths. In the old tales, people were challenged to pass through a labyrinth, and those who got lost starved to death or were attacked by a monster known as the Minotaur. Today, scientists use miniature labyrinths to experiment with mice and learn about their behavior.

It's **Norma's** twelfth birthday. This year, her family gave her a **boom box**. If every year before **were the same**, how many does she have?

One—every year is not the same!

When **Toby's** family entered the Yummyville **eating contest**, Toby was amazed when his little brother won the prize for swallowing over 1,000 items in **2** minutes. **Do you know how he did it?**

Each item was a grain of rice

Hidden Family

Can you find the family member who is hiding in each one of these sentences?

1. **We had fun cleaning the garage!**
2. **The leprechaun told me where to find a pot of gold!**
3. **The music was so raucous, I needed to cover my ears!**
4. **Under the sofa there are many dustballs.**
5. **Did you read the same memo the rest of us read?**
6. **During a crisis, terrific people often show up to help!**
7. **The chicken broth erased the last symptoms of Brian's cold.**
8. **My friend in L.A. was happy to have me visit her!**

Why did the watch go visit its parents?
It wanted to have some family "time."

What do you get when you hook a bunch of yarn together?
A close "knit" family.

What does a wrestler say when he can't say "aunt"?
Uncle.

What do you call baby jellybeans?
Sweet.

What's the difference between a brother and a bother?
An "r."

What is your father if you take his favorite chair?
A mad dad.

What is the Trampoline family's favorite time of year for vacation?
The spring.

Someone in the **Steinbeck** family plays an instrument. Can you guess which instrument? **Here's a clue:** "I have no locks, but 88 keys."

The piano

If **Lisa's** family has **1** child every **2** years and Lisa, who's the oldest, is now **11**, how many children are in her family now?

6 children

Karl and **Kate** were both in the kitchen at **1:30** for a snack, yet neither one saw the other. **How can this be?**

Karl was there at 1:30 P.M. while Kate was there at 1:30 A.M.

Try This Try This Try This

Optical Illusions
When your brain and eyes work together, sometimes they can play tricks on you. Some of these tricks are known as optical illusions. To try one optical illusion test, take 2 empty paper towel tubes and hold the end of each one up to your eyes. Keeping them straight, look through the tubes. Now, while you are still looking through them, move the ends that are farthest from your eyes together until they touch. What do you see?

Who am I?

It may "shock" you to know what I discovered—and some say I had an "electric" personality. To this day, I'm sometimes called one of the Founding Fathers, and my portrait appears on one of those green bills you use to pay for things. **Who am I?**

Benjamin Franklin

When the **Smith** family decided to move, everyone pitched in, including Sybil and her sister. If the girls can carry 2 **large** objects or 6 **small** ones each time, how many **trips** will it take to move 10 large objects and 16 small ones?

8 trips

If it takes **12** minutes for the **Gowen** family to wait for a ride on the roller coaster, and **5** minutes for everyone to get off it, how many minutes are spent screaming?

7 minutes

Jack has a lot of dishes to do. He has enough dishes to fill **4 sinks**, and it takes him **10 minutes** to wash one sinkful, **5** minutes to rinse it, and **5** minutes to dry. How much time would it save him if he waited and rinsed all the dishes at the end (**10 minutes total**), and let them all air dry?

It would save him 30 minutes

When **Marty's** dad asked him if he had been taking out the **trash** like he was supposed to, he answered, "Yes, I look at the moon every night I go out." Of course his father knew this was a lie. **Why?**

The moon is not visible every night

Words to Know

genius:

Someone who is considered to be extremely intelligent. Most people believe that geniuses are born that way and that a person can't just be taught to become a genius.

Write your own jokes here:

_____

_____

_____

_____

_____

_____

_____

_____

_____

_____

_____

_____

Chapter 10

Back in Time

Where do all the knights go to get into shape?

A knight club.

How could young George Washington have changed history forever?

By burying the hatchet.

What was King George's favorite tool?

A ruler.

What do you have if you mix a commander of a ship with a fishing lure?

Captain Hook.

What happened when Independence Hall told the Liberty Bell a joke?

It cracked up.

How can you tell when a cowboy is really upset?

He's at the end of his rope!

Who am I?

About 200 years ago, when I was known as John Chapman, I had a dream of helping to feed the hungry by planting apple trees everywhere. Some people made fun of my dream and my journeys all over America. **Who am I?**

Johnny Appleseed

I am always **stuffed** though I **never eat**. I couldn't "bear" it if I had no fur. I was named after President Theodore. **Do you know who I am?**

A teddy bear

When the **captain** climbed aboard the ship, he kept hearing dot, dot, dot, dash, dash, dash, dot, dot, dot. **Why?**

It was Morse code for S O S or "help!"

ILCU4TB47. How might history have been changed if this secret message had not been delivered before the **Boston Tea Party?**

The Boston Tea Party never would have happened—the message says, "I'll see you for tea before seven."

Words to Know

hypnosis:

A sleep-like state brought on by a hypnotist, who can direct a hypnotized person to do different things through the power of suggestion.

One day **George Washington** decided to chop down a cherry tree. After **6** swings of his axe, he managed to chop **3** inches into the tree. If the tree is **20** inches thick and he only has the energy for **36** more swings, will George be able to **cut all the way through?**

Yes, he will have chopped through 21 inches total

When the **pilgrims** landed at **Plymouth Rock**, somehow they knew what time it was. (**Hint:** They knew how to use a sundial.)

They could tell by the shadow of the rock

Lost Letters

Abe Lincoln was known for wearing a tall black hat. Use this "stovepipe" hat decoder to answer the following riddle:

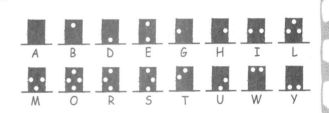

Where did Abe Lincoln have his mail delivered?

99

What was little Ben Franklin's kite-flying experience like?
Shocking!

What did Lewis and Clark say when they reached the Mississippi?
"We'll cross that bridge when they build it."

Where do "crazy" cowboys go?
To the "Wild" West.

What kind of coat has no legs?
A coat of arms.

What would Alexander Graham Bell do when he couldn't tell a person something?
He would "tell a phone."

What does Robin Hood put on all of his presents?
Bows and arrows.

Words to Know

thinking:

The process by which the brain creates ideas and makes decisions. When you are thinking of an answer to a math problem, your brain is processing the information that you have stored in your memory to find the solution.

What's **black** and **white** and **read** all over?

The Constitution

What do you get if you take off **3 weeks** in July?

¼ of July

Who am I?

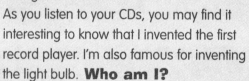

My love of music and a good challenge changed the world forever. As you listen to your CDs, you may find it interesting to know that I invented the first record player. I'm also famous for inventing the light bulb. **Who am I?**

Thomas Edison

Help!

To answer the riddle below, circle the letters that follow these rules:

- NOT a letter that sounds like the name of a bird
- NOT the last letter of the alphabet
- NOT the vowel A, O, or U

What time is it when a princess gets captured by a dragon?

As Different as Knight and Day

These two knights riding into battle might look the same, but see if you can find the 11 differences between them!

```
U  K  Z  O  J  Z      A  U  N  J  Z  A  Z     J
O     U  J  Z  O  I    A  J  O  Z  G  J  O     U
J                         Z  O  H  J  Z  O     U
A     J  Z                   Z  Z  U  A  Z     A  Z
J     O                         A  O  T  O     Z  A
Z                                              A  Z
                                    J  A       J
Z     O  Z  O     O  U                         O
T  Z  A  J  I  Z  J                             O
J  O  J  Z  J  U  J                             J
O  Z  M  J  U  A  Z        Z  E        J  Z
```

Boo Hoo!

A riddle and its answer were put into the large grid and then cut into eight pieces. See if you can figure out where each piece goes, and write the letters in their proper places. When you have filled in the grid correctly, you will be able to read the puzzle from left to right, and top to bottom. HINT: The black boxes stand for the spaces between words. Careful—some pieces are turned or flipped!

Fun Fact

Happy Tears

Have you ever thought about how laughing and crying are a lot alike? Not only do we laugh when we are happy, but we also laugh when something unexpected scares us. We cry for two reasons, too. Usually we cry when we are sad, but laughing hard may also bring tears to your eyes.

"I fly **high**, but have no wings.
I have stripes, but am no **tiger**.
I stand **strong**, though I am fragile."
What is it?

The American flag

When **Christopher Columbus** sailed to America, he wanted to prove that the earth was not flat. **How did he know he was right?**

If he was wrong, he would have sailed over the edge of the ocean.

"The **Indians** welcomed the Pilgrims to the new land." **What is wrong with that sentence?**

The land was actually very old

Who wrote the book I Can Open Any Lock?
Francis Got (Scott) Key.

What do you get if you attach a 10-foot straw to a 50-gallon vacuum?
A really big sucker.

What do you call the president's home in a blizzard?
The "white" house.

What allows ducks to be free?
The Bill of Rights.

What president won the record for doing the most laundry?
George Washing-ton.

Why did Betsy Ross sew the flag?
She didn't like to knit.

103

What did they call Edison's light bulb?

A bright idea!

What national monument requires the most cleaning?

Mount Brushmore!

Which president was really generous?

Ulysses Grant.

Why did the Berlin Wall fall?

It wanted to go down in history.

What famous philosopher had lots and lots of wagons?

Des-cart-es.

How did Betsy Ross get George Washington to stop?

She flagged him down.

What **three-letter** ending will complete all of these words? **Sail, fish, go, stay.**

–ing

"I have **ears**, but cannot hear, I can feed others but cannot **eat**. **What am I?**

Corn

Good Idea Goodies

In cartoons, a symbol for thinking or getting an idea is a light bulb. You could make some idea or light bulb cookies by using regular sugar cookie dough and cutting it out into circles. Then add a small amount of dough to the bottom of each circle shaped like the base of a light bulb. After your cookies are baked and cooled, you can frost the circle part yellow. Then you can wait to see how long it takes for someone to come up with the idea to eat them!

Who am I?

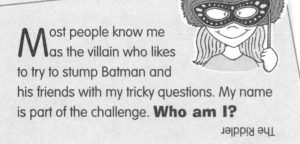

Most people know me as the villain who likes to try to stump Batman and his friends with my tricky questions. My name is part of the challenge. **Who am I?**

The Riddler

Why did the pirates walk the plank?
They were "board."

What do the pirates do when they get hungry?
They have the Captain Cook.

What president liked to dance?
James Polk-a.

When the soldiers asked the commanding officer, "Do we usually win?" how did he answer?
General Lee (generally).

Which president probably made his own suits?
Zachary Taylor.

What famous woman took the most baths?
Harriet Tubman.

How many **stripes** have been added to our **flag** over the years?

None (only stars!)

How can **Abraham Lincoln** be in many places at the same time?

He is on all the pennies and the $5 bill

History can make two words. **What are they?**

"His" and "story"

"We all are **one**, but we are **three**. We go **ashore**, but out to **sea**." **What are we?**

The Nina, the Pinta, and the Santa Maria (Christopher Columbus's ships)

Fun Fact

Secret Codes and Ciphers
Like riddles and brain teasers, codes and ciphers challenge us to think in order to find the right answer. Often, codes are used as a way of sharing information or secrets between two people. All codes come with a "key" or guide to help solve them.

Fun Fact

A Variety of Fun
Humor comes in many forms. Some people find humor in a funny or witty answer, while others like to laugh at silly stunts. Imitation is also another way to make someone laugh.

Try This

Multiple Tasking
Maybe you have heard of the term "multitasking." Multitasking means doing more than one thing at a time. Here's a challenge for you. Can you tap your foot while you bounce a tennis ball and chew gum? (Bet it's not as easy as you thought.) Can you think of any other multitasking trick to try out?

Why didn't the chariots ever stop?
They were always roamin' (Roman).

What do you call a rich retriever?
A Golden Spike.

What do you get when you cross a bison with a dollar?
A Buffalo Bill.

How do you call your pet cat and bird in North Carolina?
Here Kitty, Kitty Hawk!

What president had holes in his ears?
Franklin Pierce.

What did they hang on Main Street when the soldiers returned from the war?
A star-spangled banner.

What pilot loved to fly the most?
Amelia "Air-Heart."

Chapter 11

A Hodgepodge of Fun

Words to Know

jest:

To say or do something in a funny way. In the days of old, jesters were kind of like personal comedians who entertained the king with silly stories and juggling tricks.

What astronaut did the most weightlifting?
Neil Arm-strong.

What is the gate's favorite sport?
Fencing.

How did the golfer get his clothes pressed?
He used his "9 iron."

Why was the baby aspirin always getting into trouble with his mother?
Because he was such a little "pill."

Why did the football join in the game?
He got a "kick" out of it.

What becomes darker as it becomes lighter?

Your shadow

How can you fit a large group of people into a very small space?

Take their picture.

What has two legs but cannot walk, and has a seat but cannot sit?

A pair of pants

Try This   Try This   Try This

Guess Again!
To play this guessing game, you will need a friend who can hide a picture under several sets of matching cards. Then you guess which two cards go together, like a 10 of hearts and a 10 of diamonds. As you find the ones that match, you should be able to guess what the picture underneath is.

Fun Fact

Before Mother Goose
Although nursery rhymes are often read to children today, once they were intended more for adults. They carried secret coded riddles and messages that were meant to be understood only by certain people.

When can one **million** become nothing?

When the only 1 there leaves

When **Joe** the mechanic had fixed what he thought was *entirely* everything that was wrong with **Mrs. Low's** car, he walked around the other side only to see he had missed one other problem. Can you figure out the four-letter car part that he had missed? **Hint: Look at the italicized word.**

Tire

What makes less **noise** as its mouth gets **wider?**

A river

What could be worse than finding that someone stole your last piece of gum?
Stepping in it.

What do you call a really bad scarf?
A bad-danna (bandanna).

Why did the clock have to be fixed?
Because it went cuckoo-coo.

What kind of money can you find at the beach?
Sand dollars.

What do you get when you cross a quilt with peanut butter?
A bed spread.

Why wouldn't anyone listen to Polly anymore?
Because she went crackers.

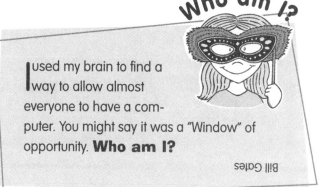

Who am I?

I used my brain to find a way to allow almost everyone to have a computer. You might say it was a "Window" of opportunity. **Who am I?**

Bill Gates

On the way home from school **Tiffany** saw a secret message written on the sidewalk: **friends just friends**. Can you guess what it means?

Just between friends

When **Emma** went to lunch with her father at a local café, somehow she felt she knew the **man** sitting near them. "I can't quite put my finger on it," she told her father. So, how did **she know** this man? Was it by his voice, his name, or his appearance? The clue is in the word **café** when you rearrange the letters.

She knew by his face

Who am I?

I have been making house calls with my books for years. My medicine is laughter. My cure is tickling your funny bone. I like to write about cats and hats. Some of my favorite things are tongue twisters and riddles. **Who am I?**

Theodore Seuss Geisel (Dr. Seuss)

Words to Know

Soothsayer:
Someone who claims to be able to "see" or predict the future. This ability to see or foresee something is considered a sixth sense. It's different from the other five senses our brain normally commands. Many people question the existence of a sixth sense.

Who won the race of the laces?
Nobody, they were tied.

Why did the aliens have to move?
They were out-er space.

How did they know the sewing machine was sick?
It just didn't seam right.

Why did the seamstress keep jumping up and down?
She was sitting on pins and needles.

How do lightning bugs see in the dark?
They use their "flash" lights.

Why did the bathtub look so tired?
Because it was really drained.

Goofy Gardener

Use the decoder to figure out the answer to this riddle:

Why did the mathematician plant his garden in milk cartons?

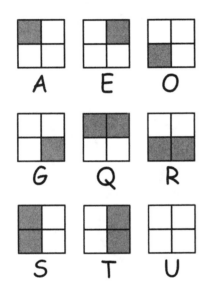

A   E   O

G   Q   R

S   T   U

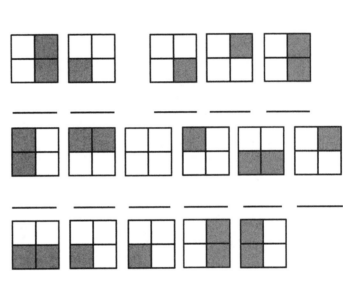

What's So Funny?

When the Williams family decided to get a swimming pool, everyone was so excited. Dad set up the pool, Mom hooked up the hose, and Junior placed it in the pool. While they were waiting for the pool to fill, they decided to go for an ice cream cone. On the way to the ice cream shop they stopped to chat with their neighbors the Smiths. An hour later someone remembered the pool. Panicked, they drove home without their ice cream, fearing the worst. **What's so funny?**

They had forgotten to turn the water on!

What **one thing** can always bring everyone down?

Gravity

What is always **coming up**, as it is always going down?

The sun

What **four letters** can bring more people to a halt than any others?

STOP

Color Me In!

Sphinx:

Words to Know

According to Greek mythology, the Sphinx was the greatest riddler of them all. This part lion–part woman kept many people puzzled with her difficult riddles.

What can **fall** without getting hurt, then always gets **back up** again?

The temperature

Just as **Heather** met the new girl, Mrs. Jones said, "No talking!" Now when would she get the chance to ask her new **friend** over to her house after school? Then it dawned on her. Do you know when she asked her? **Here's your clue: *classes in classes***

In between classes

Fun Fact

Easy as Pie
Riddles and jokes are very popular with children these days. In the past, riddles were taken rather seriously and were intended for adults only. Sometimes these riddles or messages were rolled up and baked into a pie. Sound familiar?

Let 'er Roll!

This game offers equal chances of winning to all the players, and you can have as many as six people join the game. Here is what you will need to play:

- **Piece of paper and pencil for each player**
- **Pair of dice**
- **Pennies for covering game card**

You also need to make a game card for each player. To do that, draw a five-squares-by-five-squares grid—you can use a ruler to make the lines straight, but it doesn't matter if they're wobbly.

Then, have one player read the following list of numbers:

1, 36, 9, 24, 18, 8, 6, 15, 30, 25, 10, 24, 18, 6, 3, 12, 2, 4, 12, 16, 9, 12, 16, 9, 12, 20, 6, 10

As each number is called out, each player should write it down in any one of the squares in the grid, until all the spaces are filled. Some numbers will appear twice.

Once you are done, the game can begin. Players take turn rolling the two dice, multiplying the two results, and then covering one number on the grid. **The first one to cover five squares in a row (in any direction) is the winner.**

Get to the Point!

Color every triangle in this puzzle to find the answer to the following riddle:

If you have ten cats in a box and one jumps out, how many are left?

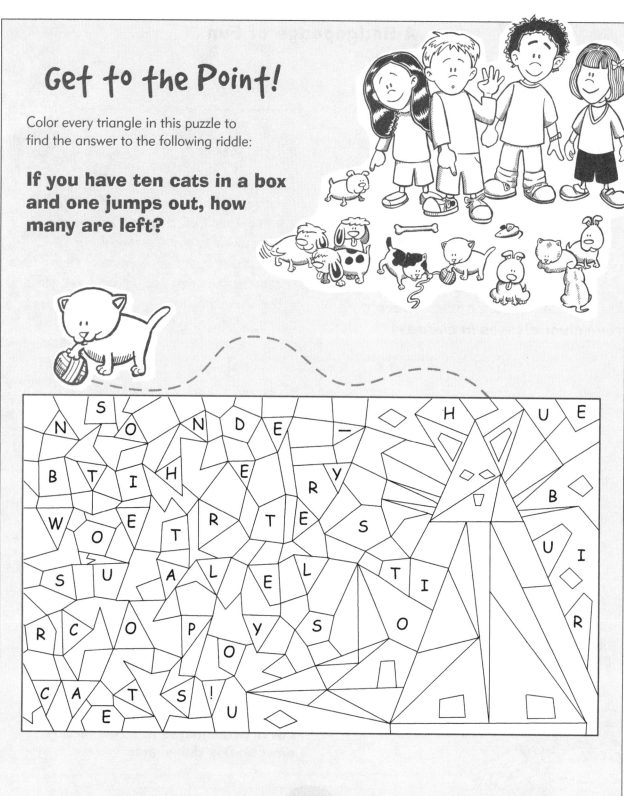

What did one shoe do to the other shoe when they got in a fight?

She socked him.

Why did the vegetables have to leave the factory?

They got canned.

Why don't trees ever go anywhere?

They don't want to "leave."

Where do ballplayers keep their money?

In "you're SAFE!"

What kind of dog loves to fight?

A boxer.

Why did the tugboat get grounded?

For barging in.

What can **hold water** no matter how many holes it has in it?

A sponge.

What never **stops** without the letter S?

A top.

Sometimes **Stu** Norticcon gets a little mixed up at his job. If you take the letters of his **name** and put them together in the right order, you will find out what kind of **job** he has.

Construction

If it takes **Stephanie** 15 minutes and 20 seconds to run 2½ miles and it takes **Trisha** 14 minutes and 83 seconds to run the same distance, who ran it the **quickest?**

Stephanie

Try This Try This Try This

It's a Guesstimate
Guessing and estimating can be lots of fun. Pour a bag of small candies into a jar. Without counting them, try to guesstimate how many there are in the jar. Now count them and see. Were you right? Next, try having someone else guesstimate how many there are. Whose guess is the closest? Can you think of other things to try and guesstimate?

What are these **three words** the beginning of? Ready, sit, go!

Musical chairs.

If all the **numbers** hold a race, how do you know who will win?

Easy, only 1 wins.

"You **bury** us though we're not **dead**, we sleep for **awhile** upon a bed, then, when we wake, we leave."
What are they?

Bulbs

Word Associations

One way to test how someone's brain works is by giving them a word association test. If I say "black," you say _____. Most would give you the opposite or the word "white." You can try this on your family and friends to see how different their answers are to these words: night, up, happy, beginning, hot, and so on.

Who am I?

Although I loved painting and became well known for my Mona Lisa, I also enjoyed inventing, studying the stars, people, and the world. Some say I was a genius. **Who am I?**

Leonardo da Vinci

What do they serve in the ocean?
Sponge cake.

What do blowfish like to chew?
Bubble gum.

How did the pig know he would make it in the movies?
He was a real ham.

Why did the throat doctor decide to quit her job?
Seeing all those tongues depressed her.

What does the zookeeper serve at snack time?
Animal crackers.

What do you get if you mix a racetrack with a circus?
A whole lot of clowning around!

How do fireflies learn their multiplication facts?

With "flash" cards.

Which number has its own day of the week?

Two's day.

How did the mountain know what it was getting for Christmas?

It peaked!

Why did the fishing pole get into trouble?

It was playing hooky.

Which month never walks?

March.

Why didn't the little fish need anyone's help in learning how to swim?

Because he could "fin" for himself.

Who am I?

I was a famous German composer. As I grew older, I lost my hearing, but I continued to write music that many people still hear quite often today. **Who am I?**

Beethoven

Words to Know

Oracle:

An oracle is a person who foretells the future using enigmas or mysterious speech. Mediums are considered oracles (or messengers) for others.

When **Xavier** the explorer finally sat down to rest, he began to wander where he was. Just then he found **four words** etched on a stone that told him the answer. The four words looked like this:

ON
OF THE WORLD

Do you know where he was?

The message means "on top of the world," so if you guessed the North Pole, you're right!

Everyone in **Kya's** family has a birthday in a month with 31 days. In how many **months** in the **year** could at least one family member be celebrating his or her birthday? Do you know which **months** they might be?

7 months—January, March, May, July, August, October, and December

Write your own jokes here:

_____

_____

_____

_____

_____

_____

_____

_____

_____

_____

_____

_____

Appendix A

Internet Resources

✐ http://blackdog4kids.com/games/word/riddles.html—BlackDog's Riddles for Kids includes riddles, games, and puzzles.

✐ http://cartooncritters.com/kidsjokes.htm—The Cartoon Critters site includes joke and riddle pages filled with tons of jokes and riddles you can share with your friends.

✐ www.eduplace.com—Education Place contains lots of resources like contests, fun online quizzes, and activities.

✐ www.fionasplace.net/Puzzlesandbrainteasers.html—Fiona's Place offers a collection of puzzles and brain teasers; some games are easy, while others are a challenge.

✐ www.humormatters.com/kidsjoke.htm—Humor Matters features jokes and riddles for kids and is updated weekly.

✐ www.justriddlesandmore.com—Just Riddles and More focuses on riddle puzzles, but also offers other types of logic and thinking puzzles.

✐ www.nationalgeographic.com/ngkids—The "Games" section of the National Geographic Kids Magazine online offers stories, games, and surprises any kid would enjoy.

✐ www.niehs.nih.gov/kids/braint.htm—NIEHS Kids Page Brainteasers, Puzzles, and Riddles, presented by the National Institute of Environmental Health Sciences, is a good way to introduce kids to environmental science, and it also includes a lot of fun games.

✐ http://pbskids.org/libertyskids—The PBS Liberty's Kids Web site offers cartoon games, word searches, and riddle riots, plus lots more.

✐ www.squiglysplayhouse.com/BrainTeasers/—Squigly's Brain Teasers for Kids offers challenging brain teasers as well as links to other puzzles, jokes, and games.

✐ http://thinks.com/brainteasers/—Thinks.com boasts 120 challenging brain teasers organized into sets of four puzzles.

696 Silly School Jokes and Riddles by Joseph Rosenbloom, New York: Sterling Publishing Co.; reprint edition, 1987.

1000 Play Thinks: Puzzles, Paradoxes, Illusions and Games by Ivan Moscovich, Ian Stewart, and Tim Robinson (Illustrator), New York: Workman Publishing Company, Spiral edition, 2001.

Are You Smart, or What? A Bizarre Book of Games and Fun for Everyone by Pasqual J. Battaglia and Pat Battaglia, Charlotte, NC: International Puzzle Features, 1st edition, 2001.

Biggest Riddle Book in the World by Joseph Rosenbloom and Joyce Behr (illustrator), New York: Sterling Publishing Co., 1983.

Calculator Riddles by David A. Adler and Cynthia Fisher (illustrator), New York: Holiday House, 1996.

Classic Brainteasers by Martin Gardner and Jeff Sinclair (illustrator), New York: Sterling Publishing Co., 1995.

The Dove Dove: Funny Homograph Riddles by Marvin Terban and Thomas Huffman (illustrator), New York: Clarion Books, 1988.

Eight Ate: A Feast of Homonym Riddles by Marvin Terban and Giulio Maestro (illustrator), Boston: Houghton Mifflin Co., 1982.

Funny You Should Ask: How to Make Up Jokes and Riddles with Wordplay by Marvin Terban and John O'Brien (illustrator), Boston: Houghton Mifflin Co., 1992.

Giggle Fit: Goofy Riddles by Joseph Rosenbloom and Steve Harpster (Author), New York: Sterling Publishing Co., 2002.

Perplexing Puzzles and Tantalizing Teasers (2 volumes in 1) by Martin Gardner and Laszlo Kubinyi (illustrator), Mineola, NY: Dover Publications, 1988.

Pun and Games: Jokes, Riddles, Rhymes, Daffynitions, Tairy Fales, and More Wordplay for Kids by Richard Lederer and Dave Morice (illustrator), Chicago: Chicago Review Press, 1996.

Rediscovered Lewis Carroll Puzzles by Lewis Carroll and Edward Wakeling (compiler), Mineola, NY: Dover Publications, 1996.

So You Think You're Smart: 150 Fun and Challenging Brain Teasers by Pat Battaglia, Charlotte, NC: International Puzzle Features, 2nd edition, 2002.

The Great Book of Mind Teasers and Mind Puzzlers by George Summers, New York: Sterling Publishing, 1986.

Too Hot to Hoot: Funny Palindrome Riddles by Marvin Terban and Giulio Maestro (illustrator), Boston: Houghton Mifflin Co., 1985.

World's Toughest Tongue Twisters by Joseph Rosenbloom and Dennis Kendrick (illustrator), New York: Sterling Publishing Co., 1987.

Appendix C

Glossary

amusement: What people do or use in order to entertain themselves or someone else. Silly or fun things are used to amuse people every day.

brain teaser: A question or test used to tease and entertain our brains. Some types of brain teasers also stimulate our funny bones. These popular little puzzles or mysteries have been around for a long time.

comedy: A type of amusement that relies on humor to entertain people. Funny stories and actions are often used in a comedy routine.

conundrum: A conundrum is a riddle that has a pun (or something with two different meanings) for the answer. Here's an example: Why was the letter B in a boat? He was going out to C. But there's another meaning to "conundrum"—it could also be a dilemma or a problem that cannot be solved.

dream: A group of thoughts, images, and feelings that you experience during the REM (rapid eye movement) portion of your sleep. Another type of dreaming is daydreaming—imagining something while you are awake.

enigma: An enigma is a phrase or question that is confusing or hard to understand. Enigmas or riddles have been used throughout time to test one's ability to solve a puzzle or mystery.

ESP: Extrasensory perception is the believed ability to have a type of sixth sense. Someone who claims to be able to read your mind or know your thoughts is said to have ESP.

genius: Someone who is considered to be extremely intelligent. Most people believe that geniuses are born that way and that a person can't just be taught to become a genius.

humor: Something that is designed to be comical or amusing. Jokes and comedy are said to be humorous, because they can make us laugh.

hypnosis: A sleeplike state brought on by a hypnotist, who can direct a hypnotized person to do different things through the power of suggestion.

IQ: IQ or Intelligence Quotient is a measure of one's ability to think. An IQ test allows people to measure genius as well as normal thinking ability.

jest: To say or do something in a funny way. In the days of old, jesters were kind of like personal comedians who entertained the king with silly stories and juggling tricks.

joke: A joke is an act or statement that causes laughter.

memory: Ability to store information in your brain. Without your memory, you could never remember your brother's birthday or where you put your favorite book. And did you know that memory is one of the things required for laughter?

oracle: An oracle is a person who foretells the future using enigmas or mysterious speech. Mediums are considered oracles (or messengers) for others.

pun: A pun is a play on words using two meanings of the same word or two words that sound the same but are spelled differently. For example, the word "sew" in the following joke: "Why do I have to?" the little sewing machine asked his mother. "Because I said SEW!"

puzzle: A type of test or challenge sometimes used to confuse someone. Often puzzles are used for learning in school settings, such as language or math lessons. Other types of puzzles are actually objects or games.

rebus: A kind of puzzle in which pictures represent words or parts of words. Sometimes a rebus will be used in a storybook to introduce new words, or in a game to challenge the guesser to solve the picture puzzle.

riddle: A question or event of puzzling nature that requires you to think of an answer. Some riddles are a type of joke. Other riddles are very serious.

sarcasm: Humorous comments made with an ironic tone. People may use sarcasm to make a negative point, but sometimes sarcasm is mistaken for a real compliment.

sense: The ability to see, smell, hear, touch, and taste all of the things that you come in contact with are made possible by your 5 senses. Your brain relies on the senses to perceive the outside world.

soothsayer: Someone who claims to be able to "see" or predict the future. This ability to see or foresee something is considered a sixth sense. It's different from the other 5 senses our brain normally commands. Many people question the existence of a sixth sense.

sphinx: According to Greek mythology, the Sphinx was the greatest riddler of them all. This part lion–part woman kept many people puzzled with her difficult riddles.

teasing: Teasing is bothering, annoying, or taunting others by making fun of them. Some teasing is just for fun—nothing to get offended about—but sometimes teasing becomes mean and should be stopped.

thinking: The process by which the brain creates ideas and makes decisions. When you are thinking of an answer to a math problem, your brain is processing the information that you have stored in your memory to find the solution.

tongue twister: A word or phrase that is hard to repeat quickly due to the repetition of multiple consonants within the words.

PUZZLE ANSWERS

page 6 • **Bad Band**

Why was the music teacher so
angry during class each day?

1E B	2F E	3H C	4F A	5A U	6B S	7E E		8F T	9G H	10D E

BECAUSE THE

STUDENTS

WERE ALWAYS

PASSING

NOTES!

A. The center of our
solar system

S U N
40 5 16

B. Covered with soap

S O A P Y
6 37 23 29 27

C. Melodies

T U N E S
12 13 34 20 18

D. Many of these
make a forest

T R E E S
38 21 10 39 28

E. Pleads

B E G S
1 7 35 11

F. Your skin will do
this on a hot day

S W E A T
31 19 2 4 8

G. To put out of sight

H I D E
9 33 14 15

H. Opposite of dirty

C L E A N
3 24 22 26 36

I. How you hit a fly

S W A T
32 25 30 17

page 8 • **A Sloppy Subject**

When should kids
wear bibs in school?

DURING A
SPILLING BEE!

page 11 • **Math Class**

*What do you get when you add 2 bananas,
1 apple, 15 grapes, and 1/2 melon?*

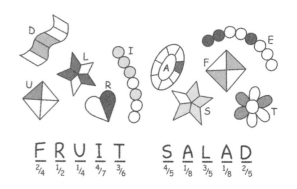

F R U I T   S A L A D
2/4 1/2 1/4 4/7 3/6   4/5 1/8 3/5 1/8 2/5

page 16 • **Loop the Zoo**

Answers: A panda rolling down a hill,
or a penguin stuck in a dryer,
or a zebra chasing his tail!

PUZZLE ANSWERS

page 19 • Say What?

C R A B	"I'm grouchy!"
P A N D A	"Where's the bamboo?"
C U B	"I'll grow up to be a big bear!"
M O N K E Y	"Got a banana?"
C R O C	"-odile is the last part of my name!"
H Y E N A	"Ha, Ha, Ha!"
W O R M	"You won't like me in your apple!"
S N A K E	"What'ssssss up?"
O W L	"Whoooo's there?"
B A T S	"Turn out the light! We like the dark!"

page 21 • Feel Better

W	H	A	T	'	S		G	R	A	Y		A	N	D
	B	R	I	N	G	S		F	L	O	W	E	R	S
	T	O		S	I	C	K		A	N	I	M	A	L
S		A	T		T	H	E		Z	O	O	?		A
G	E	T	-	W	E	L	L	E	P	H	A	N	T	!

page 27 • Funny Flight

"I just flew home from Paris, and..."

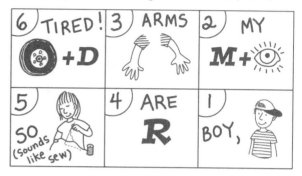

page 28 • Where in the World?

1. Where do fish go on vacation? **Finland**
2. Where do songbirds go on vacation? **The Canary Islands**
3. Where do zombies go on vacation? **The Dead Sea**
4. Where do Thanksgiving birds go on vacation? **Turkey**
5. Where do geometry teachers go on vacation? **Cuba**
6. Where do locksmiths go on vacation? **The Florida Keys**

PUZZLE ANSWERS

page 31 • The Hungry Traveler

A h<u>u</u>n<u>gry</u> tra<u>ve</u>l<u>er</u> <u>was</u> taking a dri<u>v</u>e throu<u>g</u>h the <u>c</u>ountry <u>s</u>ide. He had <u>brou</u>g<u>h</u>t a <u>sal</u>ad <u>with</u> hi<u>m</u>, <u>b</u>ut forgot an im<u>p</u>ortant too<u>l</u>. The hungry tra<u>ve</u>l<u>er</u> fig<u>u</u>red he <u>cou</u>l d eat <u>lunc</u>h <u>w</u>hen he got to a <u>c</u>ertain kind of inter<u>se</u>ction. <u>W</u>hat <u>was</u> the h<u>u</u>n<u>gry</u> tra<u>ve</u>l<u>er</u> <u>w</u>aiting for?

<u>A F O R K I N T H E R O A D</u>!

page 37 • Frightened Food

Answer: A CHICKEN SANDWICH

page 38 • Good Home Cookin'

Where does a snail like to eat lunch?

<u>IN A SLOW FOOD RESTAURANT</u>!

page 40 • Second Helping

1.	A	L	B	I	N	O	S
2.	A	Q	U	A	T	I	C
3.	C	A	R	M	I	N	E
4.	C	O	N	S	E	N	T
5.	C	O	T	T	A	G	E
6.	E	S	T	U	A	R	Y
7.	G	O	O	F	U	P	S
8.	L	O	A	F	E	R	S
9.	M	I	S	E	R	L	Y
10.	O	U	T	D	O	O	R

130

PUZZLE ANSWERS

page 46 • Comic Contest

1. baseball cap, weather balloons, sweat-R (sweater), pet sheepdog
2. stocking cap, pet hot dog, blue (sad) jeans, pair of slippers (otherwise known as banana peels)
3. top hat, T-shirt, pet watchdog
4. THE WINNER! ski hat, rain coat, seeing i (eye) dog, bellbottom pants, elevator shoes

page 49 • Silly Sally

Silly Sally like things that have double letters! Look at the picture of Silly Sally and you will see a balloon, a butterfly, glasses, earrings, mittens, buttons, a dress (covered with loops), boots, and a poodle!

page 50 • Silly Slogans

1. Top Card Playing Company "Come see us when you...	want a good deal!
2. B&B Baking and Loan "Come see us when you...	knead dough!
3. Al's Barber Shop "Come see us when you...	are in a hurry. We know all the short cuts!
4. Larry's Lightbulbs "Come see us when you...	need a bright idea!
5. Elegant Eyewear "Come see us when you...	want to look better!
6. Good Deal Real Estate "Come see us when you...	are looking for a yard sale!

page 55 • Cross Plumber

What do you get when you cross a plumber with a jeweler?

A RING AROUND THE BATHTUB!

page 56 • Why Did the Lion...

Answer: To get to the other pride!

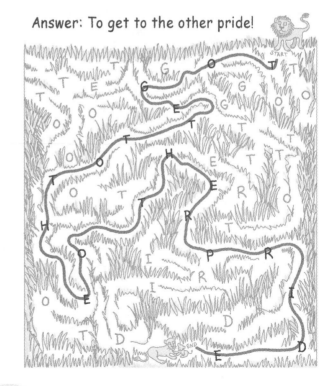

131

PUZZLE ANSWERS

page 59 • **Hinky Pinkies**

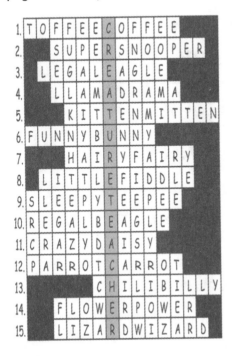

1. TOFFEE COFFEE
2. SUPER SNOOPER
3. LEGAL EAGLE
4. LLAMA DRAMA
5. KITTEN MITTEN
6. FUNNY BUNNY
7. HAIRY FAIRY
8. LITTLE FIDDLE
9. SLEEPY TEEPEE
10. REGAL BEAGLE
11. CRAZY DAISY
12. PARROT CARROT
13. CHILI BILLY
14. FLOWER POWER
15. LIZARD WIZARD

page 69 • **Which Window?**

Answer: The outside!

page 70 • **Fun House**

The answer to the riddle is upside down and backwards!

page 66 • **Half a House?**

What kind of house does every house builder know how to build?

C-2	H+6	J-5	Z-3	K+4	S-5	B+3
A	N	E	W	O	N	E

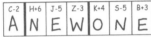

PUZZLE ANSWERS

page 78 • **Night Games**

Which animals are always invited to night baseball games?

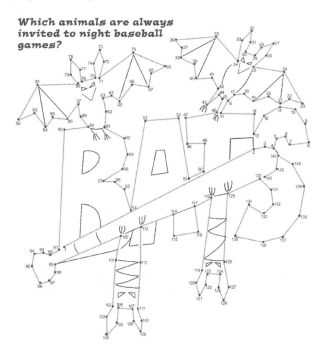

page 81 • **hOops**

A. <u>S H Y</u> Easily frighened; timid
   10 2 7

B. <u>B R I D E</u> Woman on her wedding day
   20 9 19 17 3

C. <u>W E B</u> What a spider builds
   13 8 21

D. <u>L A Y E R</u> One thickness of something
   5 11 15 23 18

E. <u>P A</u> Short nickname for father
   4 14

F. <u>S T A L L</u> Place in a barn for a horse
   16 1 6 12 22

Why is a basketball court often wet?

THE PLAYERS ALWAYS DRIBBLE!

page 82 • **Balls of Fun**

1. SOALCRSE   LACROSSE
2. IFEDL OHCKYE   FIELD HOCKEY
3. GOIWLBN   BOWLING
4. NPIG OGPN   PING PONG
5. USQSAH   SQUASH
6. OOPL   POOL (or POLO)
7. ENITNS   TENNIS
8. FOLG   GOLF
9. ROCUQET   CROQUET
10. OPLO   POLO (or POOL)

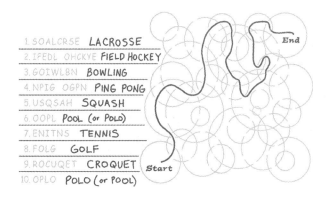

page 89 • **Big Brothers**

Starting in the lower righthand corner, going up, then spiraling around: The Woods have six children, five boys and one girl. Any one of the boys will have four brothers, while the girl will have five brothers.

D	L	I	H	C	X	I	S	E
R	O	B	E	H	T	F	O	V
E	Y	L	I	H	W	S	E	A
N	S	E	I	F	E	R	N	H
F	W	T	V	S	V	E	O	S
I	I	H	E	R	A	H	Y	D
V	L	E	B	E	H	T	N	O
E	L	G	R	H	L	O	A	O
B	H	I	O	T	L	R	L	W
O	A	R	L	W	I	B	R	E
Y	V	E	F	O	U	R	I	H
S	A	N	D	O	N	E	G	T

PUZZLE ANSWERS

page 90 • The Family Name Game

8.
Mrs. Cathy

1. Mrs. Patti				P	A	N	C	A	K	E		
2. Mrs. Frieda	F	L	Y	P	A	P	E	R				
3. Mrs. Fran			F	I	R	E	W	O	O	D		
4. Mrs. Paula		P	I	G	P	E	N					
5. Mrs. Carol			C	O	O	K	B	O	O	K		
6. Mrs. Fiona			F	O	O	T	B	A	L	L		
7. Mrs. Rachel	R	A	T	T	L	E	S	N	A	K	E	

page 92 • Watch Out! Answer 1

	I	T̶				O	H		
	D	A	T		Y	A	U		
D	H̶	N	E		X̶	T	R̶	A	
B̶	I	O	X̶	S	S	G̶	A	T	Y
T	O	T	G	M	I	T	T	X̶	L
D	O	N'T			P	A	T		
T	H	A	T		S	T	R	A	Y
	D	O	G'S		T	A	I	L	
—	I	T			M	I	G	H	T
B	I	T	E		Y	O	U		!

page 92 • Watch Out! Answer 2

	X̶	T	G			N	E		E		
	O	Ø	M			W̶	O	V̶	R	R	
B	M	R	T		W̶	O	F̶	R	S	H̶	
D	D	Ø	T		O	F̶	R	S	H̶		
P̶	A	N	E	S	T	H	X̶	T	Y	E	
D	O	N'T			W	O	R	R	Y		
	M	O	M	—	T	H	I	S			
P	A	R	T		O	F		T	H	E	
	D	O	G		N	E	V	E	R		
B	I	T	E	S	!						

page 93 • Hidden Family

1. We had f**un cle**aning the garage!
2. The leprech**aun t**old me where to find a pot of gold!
3. The music was so rau**cous, I n**eeded to cover my ears!
4. Under the so**fa ther**e are many dustballs.
5. Did you read the same me**mo the r**est of us read?
6. During a cri**sis, ter**rific people often show up to help!
7. The chicken **broth er**ased the last symptoms of Brian's cold.
8. My friend **in L.A. w**as happy to have me visit her!

PUZZLE ANSWERS

page 99 • Lost Letters

Where did Abe Lincoln have his mail delivered?

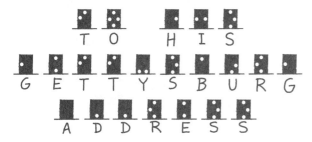

T O   H I S

G E T T Y S B U R G

A D D R E S S

page 101 • Help and **As Different as Knight and Day**

Answer:
KNIGHT TIME!

page 102 • Boo Hoo!

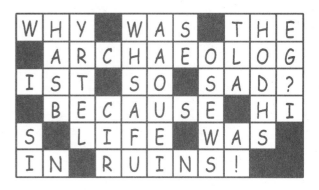

W	H	Y		W	A	S		T	H	E
	A	R	C	H	A	E	O	L	O	G
I	S	T		S	O		S	A	D	?
	B	E	C	A	U	S	E		H	I
S		L	I	F	E		W	A	S	
I	N		R	U	I	N	S	!		

page 111 • Goofy Gardener

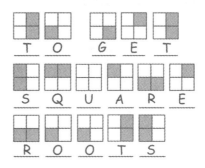

T O   G E T

S Q U A R E

R O O T S

page 114 • Get to the Point!

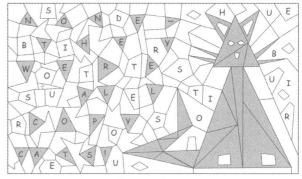

Answer: None — they were all copy cats!

 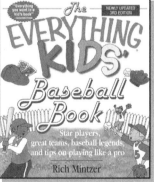

The Everything® Kids' Bugs Book
    1-58062-892-3

The Everything® Kids' Christmas Puzzle &
    Activity Book 1-58062-965-2

The Everything® Kids' Cookbook
    1-58062-658-0

The Everything® Kids' Halloween Puzzle &
    Activity Book 1-58062-959-8

The Everything® Kids' Joke Book
    1-58062-686-6

The Everything® Kids' Math Puzzles Book
    1-58062-773-0

The Everything® Kids' Monsters Book
    1-58062-657-2

The Everything® Kids' Mazes Book
    1-58062-558-4

The Everything® Kids' Money Book
    1-58062-685-8 ($11.95 CAN)

The Everything® Kids' Nature Book
    1-58062-684-X ($11.95 CAN)

The Everything® Kids' Puzzle Book
    1-58062-687-4

The Everything® Kids' Science Experiments Book
    1-58062-557-6

The Everything® Kids' Soccer Book
    1-58062-642-4

The Everything® Kids' Travel Activity Book
    1-58062-641-6

All Kids' titles are priced at $6.95 ($10.95 CAN) unless otherwise noted.

OTHER *EVERYTHING*® BOOKS BY ADAMS MEDIA

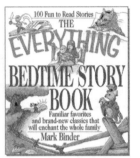

Trade Paperback, $14.95
1-58062-147-3, 304 pages

The Everything® Bedtime Story Book
by Mark Binder

The Everything® Bedtime Story Book is a wonderfully original collection of 100 stories that will delight the entire family. Accompanied by charming illustrations, the stories included are retold in an exceptionally amusing style and are perfect for reading aloud. From familiar nursery rhymes to condensed American classics, this collection promises to promote sweet dreams, active imaginations, and quality family time.

The Everything® Mother Goose Book
by June Rifkin

The Everything® Mother Goose Book is a delightful collection of 300 nursery rhymes that will entertain adults and children alike. These wonderful rhymes are easy for even young readers to enjoy—and great for reading aloud. Each page is decorated with captivating drawings of beloved characters. Ideal for any age, *The Everything® Mother Goose Book* will inspire young readers and take parents on an enchanting trip down memory lane.

Trade Paperback, $12.95
1-58062-490-1, 304 pages

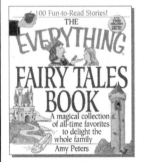

Trade Paperback, $12.95
1-58062-546-0, 304 pages

The Everything® Fairy Tales Book
by Amy Peters

Take your children to magical lands where animals talk, mythical creatures wander freely, and good and evil come in every imaginable form. You'll find all this and more in *The Everything® Fairy Tales Book*, an extensive collection of 100 classic fairy tales. This enchanting compilation features charming, original illustrations that guarantee creative imaginations and quality family time.

Available wherever books are sold!
To order, call 800-872-5627, or visit us at everything.com

Everything® and everything.com® are registered trademarks of F+W Publications, Inc.